To:

_____

From:

_____

God's Inspirational Promises

MAX LUCADO

COUNTRYMAN ®

A Division of Thomas Nelson Publishers

THOMAS NELSON

Since 1798

NASHVILLE   DALLAS   MEXICO CITY   RIO DE JANEIRO

Published in Nashville, Tennessee, by Thomas Nelson. Thomas Nelson is a registered trademark of Thomas Nelson, Inc.

Thomas Nelson, Inc., titles may be purchased in bulk for educational, business, fund-raising, or sales promotional use. For information, please e-mail SpecialMarkets@ThomasNelson.com.

ISBN: 978-1-4041-7486-3
ISBN: 978-0-529-12085-4 (CU)

Printed in China

14 15 16 17 18 TIMS 5 4 3 2 1

Contents

Inspirational
Promises
to Give Insight

COURAGE

Could you use some courage? Are you backing down more than you are standing up? Jesus scattered the butterflies out of the stomachs of his nervous disciples.

We need to remember that the disciples were common men given a compelling task. Before they were the stained-glassed saints in the windows of cathedrals, they were somebody's next-door neighbors trying to make a living and raise a family. They weren't cut from theological cloth or raised on supernatural milk. But they were an ounce more devoted than they were afraid and, as a result, did some extraordinary things.

Earthly fears are no fears at all. Answer the big question of eternity, and the little questions of life fall into perspective.

The Applause of Heaven

Let your words of hope and the promise of a glorious future in your kingdom give me hope and courage for today, Father. You are with me now as you will be throughout all eternity.

Inspirational Promises

"Don't be afraid, because I have saved you. I have called you by name, and you are mine. When you pass through the waters, I will be with you. When you cross rivers, you will not drown. When you walk through fire, you will not be burned, nor will the flames hurt you. This is because I, the Lord, am your God, the Holy One of Israel, your Savior."

Isaiah 43:1–3

"Don't worry, because I am with you. Don't be afraid, because I am your God. I will make you strong and will help you; I will support you with my right hand that saves you. . . . I am the Lord your God, who holds your right hand, and I tell you, 'Don't be afraid. I will help you.'"

Isaiah 41:10, 13

How great is your goodness that you have stored up for those who fear you, that you have given to those who trust you. You do this for all to see. You protect them by your presence from what people plan against them. You shelter them from evil words.

Psalm 31:19–20

FAITH

Faith is the belief that God is real and that God is good. . . . It is a choice to believe that the one who made it all hasn't left it all and that he still sends light into the shadows and responds to gestures of faith.

Faith is the belief that God will do what is right.

God says that the more hopeless your circumstances, the more likely your salvation. The greater your cares, the more genuine your prayers. The darker the room, the greater the need for light.

God's help is near and always available, but it is only given to those who seek it.

He Still Moves Stones

Father, we long to submit ourselves to you so that we will know the holy freedom only you can give. Thank you for giving us hope and strength even when our faith is small.

INSPIRATIONAL PROMISES

Faith means being sure of the things we hope for and knowing that something is real even if we do not see it. . . . It is by faith we understand that the whole world was made by God's command so what we see was made by something that cannot be seen. . . . Without faith no one can please God. Anyone who comes to God must believe that he is real and that he rewards those who truly want to find him.

Hebrews 11:1, 3, 6

The Good News shows how God makes people right with himself—that it begins and ends with faith. As the Scripture says, "But those who are right with God will live by trusting in him."

Romans 1:17

We have troubles all around us, but we are not defeated. We do not know what to do, but we do not give up the hope of living. We are persecuted, but God does not leave us. We are hurt sometimes, but we are not destroyed. . . . So we do not give up. Our physical body is becoming older and weaker, but our spirit inside us is made new every day. We have small troubles for a while now, but they are helping us gain an eternal glory that is much greater than the troubles. We set our eyes not on what we see but on what we cannot see.

2 Corinthians 4:8–9, 16–18

CONTENTMENT

Satisfied? That is one thing we are not. We are not satisfied.

We take a vacation of a lifetime. . . . We satiate ourselves with sun, fun, and good food. But we are not even on the way home before we dread the end of the trip and begin planning another.

We are not satisfied.

As a child we say, "If only I were a teenager." As a teen we say, "If only I were an adult." As an adult, "If only I were married." As a spouse, "If only I had kids."

We are not satisfied. Contentment is a difficult virtue. Why?

Because there is nothing on earth that can satisfy our deepest longing. We long to see God. The leaves of life are rustling with the rumor that we will—and we won't be satisfied until we do.

When God Whispers Your Name

Father, keep us from being so blinded by possessions we cannot keep that we fail to see the eternal treasure we cannot lose.

Serving God does make us very rich, if we are satisfied with what we have. We brought nothing into the world, so we can take nothing out. But, if we have food and clothes, we will be satisfied with that. Those who want to become rich bring temptation to themselves and are caught in a trap. They want many foolish and harmful things that ruin and destroy people. The love of money causes all kinds of evil. Some people have left the faith, because they wanted to get more money, but they have caused themselves much sorrow.

1 Timothy 6:6–10

Do not worry about anything, but pray and ask God for everything you need, always giving thanks. And God's peace, which is so great we cannot understand it, will keep your hearts and minds in Christ Jesus. . . . I have learned to be satisfied with the things I have and with everything that happens. I know how to live when I am poor, and I know how to live when I have plenty. I have learned the secret of being happy at any time in everything that happens. . . . I can do all things through Christ, because he gives me strength.

Philippians 4:6–7, 11–13

LOVE

The single most difficult pursuit is truth and love.

That sentence is grammatically correct. I know every English teacher would like to pluralize it to read: The most difficult pursuits are those of truth and love. But that's not what I mean to say.

Love is a difficult pursuit.

Truth is a tough one too.

But put them together, pursue truth and love at the same time and hang on, baby, you're in for the ride of your life.

Love in truth. Truth in love. Never one at the expense of the other. Never the embrace of love without the torch of truth. Never the heat of truth without the warmth of love.

To pursue both is our singular task.

The Inspirational Study Bible

God of heaven, we see your hand stretching as far as the east is from the west. Put your hands and your arms around us and embrace us, Father. Then help us to stretch out our hands and arms to a world that desperately needs your love—and ours.

Love is patient and kind. Love is not jealous, it does not brag, and it is not proud. Love is not rude, is not selfish, and does not get upset with others. Love does not count up wrongs that have been done. Love takes no pleasure in evil but rejoices over the truth. Love patiently accepts all things. It always trusts, always hopes, and always endures.

1 Corinthians 13:4–7

We know the love that God has for us, and we trust that love. God is love. Those who live in love live in God, and God lives in them.

1 John 4:16

"The Father himself loves you. He loves you because you loved me and believed that I came from God."

John 16:27

"I give you a new command: Love each other. You must love each other as I have loved you. All people will know that you are my followers if you love each other."

John 13:34–35

HOPE

It's hard to see things grow old. The town in which I grew up is growing old. . . . Some of the buildings are boarded up. Some of the houses are torn down. . . . The old movie house where I took my dates has "For Sale" on the marquee.

I wish I could make it all new again. I wish I could blow the dust off the streets . . . but I can't.

I can't. But God can. "He restores my soul," wrote the shepherd. God doesn't reform; he restores. He doesn't camouflage the old; he restores the new. The Master Builder will pull out the original plan and restore it. He will restore the vigor. He will restore the energy. He will restore the hope. He will restore the soul.

The Applause of Heaven

You never promised us that this world would be easy. And yet all of us can look ahead to the city that's set on a hill, to the lights that call us to eternity. And we take hope.

INSPIRATIONAL PROMISES

No king is saved by his great army. No warrior escapes by his great strength. . . . But the LORD looks after those who fear him, those who put their hope in his love. He saves them from death and spares their lives in times of hunger. So our hope is in the LORD. He is our help, our shield to protect us.

Psalm 33:16, 18–20

If God is with us, no one can defeat us. He did not spare his own Son but gave him for us all. So with Jesus, God will surely give us all things. Who can accuse the people God has chosen? No one, because God is the One who makes them right.

Romans 8:31–33

The LORD's love never ends; his mercies never stop. They are new every morning; LORD, your loyalty is great. I say to myself, "The LORD is mine, so I hope in him." The LORD is good to those who hope in him, to those who seek him.

Lamentations 3:22–25

TRUTH

Imagine that you are an ice skater in competition. You are in first place with one more round to go. If you perform well, the trophy is yours. You are nervous, anxious, and frightened.

Then, only minutes before your performance, your trainer rushes to you with the thrilling news: "You've already won! The judges tabulated the scores, and the person in second place can't catch you. You are too far ahead."

Upon hearing that news, how will you feel? Exhilarated!

And how will you skate? . . . How about courageously and confidently? You bet you will. You will do your best because the prize is yours.

The point is clear: the truth will triumph. The Father of truth will win, and the followers of truth will be saved.

The Applause of Heaven

Father, thank you for your truth. Help us to see what is important, what is eternal, and what is lasting. Help us to put into practice the timeless truths found in your Word.

The teachings of the LORD are perfect; they give new strength. The rules of the LORD can be trusted; they make plain people wise. . . . The judgments of the LORD are true; they are completely right.

Psalm 19:7, 9

How I love your teachings! I think about them all day long. Your commands make me wiser than my enemies, because they are mine forever. . . . Your words are true from the start, and all your laws will be fair forever.

Psalm 119:97–98, 160

We also know that the Son of God has come and has given us understanding so that we can know the True One. And our lives are in the True One and in his Son, Jesus Christ. He is the true God and the eternal life.

1 John 5:20

STRENGTH

An example of faith was found on the wall of a concentration camp. On it a prisoner had carved the words:

I believe in the sun, even though it doesn't shine,
I believe in love, even when it isn't shown,
I believe in God, even when he doesn't speak.

I try to imagine the person who etched those words. I try to envision his skeletal hand gripping the broken glass or stone that cut into the wall. I try to imagine his eyes squinting through the darkness as he carved each letter. What hand could have cut such a conviction? What eyes could have seen good in such horror?

There is only one answer: eyes that chose to see the unseen.

He Still Moves Stones

Father, you promised us faith and strength and hope to meet life's problems. Please give that strength to those whose anxieties have buried their dreams, whose illnesses have hospitalized their hopes, whose burdens are bigger than their shoulders.

He gives strength to those who are tired and more power to those who are weak. . . . But the people who trust the LORD will become strong again. They will rise up as an eagle in the sky; they will run and not need rest; they will walk and not become tired.

Isaiah 40:29, 31

"Come to me, all of you who are tired and have heavy loads, and I will give you rest. Accept my teachings and learn from me, because I am gentle and humble in spirit, and you will find rest for your lives. The teaching that I ask you to accept is easy; the load I give you to carry is light."

Matthew 11:28–30

God is our protection and our strength. He always helps in times of trouble. . . . The LORD All-Powerful is with us; the God of Jacob is our defender.

Psalm 46:1, 11

PATIENCE

God is often more patient with us than we are with ourselves. We assume that if we fall, we aren't born again. If we stumble, then we aren't truly converted. If we have the old desires, then we must not be a new creation.

If you are anxious about this, please remember, "God began doing a good work in you, and I am sure he will continue it until it is finished when Jesus Christ comes again" (Philippians 1:6).

A Gentle Thunder

I am encouraged when I think of your patience, Father, and of your unfailing love. Help me to be patient—with people, with circumstances, even with myself.

We also have joy with our troubles, because we know that these troubles produce patience. And patience produces character, and character produces hope. And this hope will never disappoint us, because God has poured out his love to fill our hearts.

Romans 5:3–5

We are surrounded by a great cloud of people whose lives tell us what faith means. So let us run the race that is before us and never give up. We should remove from our lives anything that would get in the way and the sin that so easily holds us back. Let us look only to Jesus, the One who began our faith and who makes it perfect.

Hebrews 12:1–2

My brothers and sisters, when you have many kinds of troubles, you should be full of joy, because you know that these troubles test your faith, and this will give you patience. Let your patience show itself perfectly in what you do. Then you will be perfect and complete and will have everything you need.

James 1:2–4

Inspirational
Promises
About God

God's Love

My child's feelings are hurt. I tell her she's special.

My child is injured. I do whatever it takes to make her feel better.

My child is afraid. I won't go to sleep until she is secure.

I'm not a hero. . . . I'm a parent. When a child hurts, a parent does what comes naturally. He helps.

Why don't I let my Father do for me what I am more than willing to do for my own children?

I'm learning. . . . Being a father is teaching me that when I am criticized, injured, or afraid, there is a Father who is ready to comfort me. There is a Father who will hold me until I'm better, help me until I can live with the hurt, and who won't go to sleep when I'm afraid of waking up and seeing the dark.

Ever.

The Applause of Heaven

Father, we look at your plan and see a plan based on love, not on our performance. Help us to be captivated by your love.

INSPIRATIONAL PROMISES

We are completely victorious through God who showed his love for us. Yes, I am sure that neither death, nor life, nor angels, nor ruling spirits, nothing now, nothing in the future, no powers, nothing above us, nothing below us, nor anything else in the whole world will ever be able to separate us from the love of God that is in Christ Jesus our Lord.

Romans 8:37–39

When we were unable to help ourselves, at the right time, Christ died for us, although we were living against God. . . . God shows his great love for us in this way: Christ died for us while we were still sinners.

Romans 5:6, 8

Lord God All-Powerful, who is like you? Lord, you are powerful and completely trustworthy. . . . Your kingdom is built on what is right and fair. Love and truth are in all you do.

Psalm 89:8, 14

GOD'S MERCY

God does not save us because of what we've done. Only a puny god could be bought with tithes. Only an egotistical god would be impressed with our pain. Only a temperamental god could be satisfied by sacrifices. Only a heartless god would sell salvation to the highest bidders.

And only a great God does for his children what they can't do for themselves.

God's delight is received upon surrender, not awarded upon conquest. The first step to joy is a plea for help, an acknowledgment of moral destitution, an admission of inward paucity. Those who taste God's presence have declared spiritual bankruptcy and are aware of their spiritual crisis. . . . Their pockets are empty. Their options are gone. They have long since stopped demanding justice; they are pleading for mercy.

The Applause of Heaven

Father, you have expressed toward us unlimited mercy. The only reason this world continues is because you have mercy upon us. Thank you for the unimaginable gifts of your love.

The Lord passed in front of Moses and said, "I am the Lord. The Lord is a God who shows mercy, who is kind, who doesn't become angry quickly, who has great love and faithfulness and is kind to thousands of people."

Exodus 34:6–7

God will show his mercy forever and ever to those who worship and serve him.

Luke 1:50

God's mercy is great, and he loved us very much. Though we were spiritually dead because of the things we did against God, he gave us new life with Christ. You have been saved by God's grace.

Ephesians 2:4–5

GOD'S FAITHFULNESS

We are God's idea. We are his. His face. His
eyes. His hands. His touch. We are him. Look deeply into
the face of every human being on earth, and you will see
his likeness. Though some appear to be distant relatives,
they are not. God has no cousins, only children.

We are, incredibly, the body of Christ. And though we
may not act like our Father, there is no greater truth than
this: We are his. Unalterably. He loves us. Undyingly.
Nothing can separate us from the love of Christ (Romans
8:38–39).

A Gentle Thunder

Father, forgive us for the times that we have questioned
you; forgive us for the times we have doubted you;
forgive us for the times we've shaken our heads and
pounded our fists against the earth and cried, "Where
are you?" For, Father, we know that you have been
here—you've carried us through the valley, and you've
given us strength.

INSPIRATIONAL PROMISES

I will always sing about the LORD's love; I will tell of his loyalty from now on. I will say, "Your love continues forever; your loyalty goes on and on like the sky."

Psalm 89:1–2

So know that the LORD your God is God, the faithful God. He will keep his agreement of love for a thousand lifetimes for people who love him and obey his commands.

Deuteronomy 7:9

Jesus will keep you strong until the end so that there will be no wrong in you on the day our Lord Jesus Christ comes again. God, who has called you into fellowship with his Son, Jesus Christ our Lord, is faithful.

1 Corinthians 1:8–9

GOD'S FORGIVENESS

When Jesus told us to pray for forgiveness of our debts as we forgive our own debtors, he knew who would be the one to pay the debt. As he would hang on the cross, he would say, "It is finished" . . . the debt is paid!

There are some facts that will never change. One fact is that you are forgiven. If you are in Christ, when he sees you, your sins are covered—he doesn't see them. He sees you better than you see yourself. And that is a glorious fact of your life.

Walking with the Savior

Sometimes we're afraid that we've done something unforgivable, afraid that we've made you angry, Father. And we wonder how you can forgive us. But, Father, your Word teaches us that you will forgive us and that there is no sin too deep for your hand of forgiveness to reach.

Inspirational Promises

The Lord says, "Come, let us talk about these things. Though your sins are like scarlet, they can be as white as snow. Though your sins are deep red, they can be white like wool."

Isaiah 1:18

Happy is the person whose sins are forgiven, whose wrongs are pardoned. Happy is the person whom the Lord does not consider guilty and in whom there is nothing false.

Psalm 32:1–2

If we confess our sins, he will forgive our sins, because we can trust God to do what is right. He will cleanse us from all the wrongs we have done.

1 John 1:9

God's Comfort

There are historical moments in which a real God met real pain so we could answer the question, "Where is God when I hurt?"

How does God react to dashed hopes? Read the story of Jairus. How does the Father feel about those who are ill? Stand with him at the pool of Bethesda. Do you long for God to speak to your lonely heart? Then listen as he speaks to the Emmaus-bound disciples.

He's not doing it just for them. He's doing it for me. He's doing it for you.

The God who spoke still speaks. . . . The God who came still comes. He comes into our world. He comes into your world. He comes to do what you can't.

He Still Moves Stones

Father, you are God and Creator, but we come to you as children coming to their father, as children who would ask their father to hold and comfort them.

Inspirational Promises

The LORD hears good people when they cry out to him, and he saves them from all their troubles. The LORD is close to the brokenhearted, and he saves those whose spirits have been crushed.

Psalm 34:17–18

God is the Father who is full of mercy and all comfort. He comforts us every time we have trouble, so when others have trouble, we can comfort them with the same comfort God gives us. We share in the many sufferings of Christ. In the same way, much comfort comes to us through Christ.

2 Corinthians 1:3–5

Even if I walk through a very dark valley, I will not be afraid, because you are with me. Your rod and your shepherd's staff comfort me.

Psalm 23:4

God's Blessings

To recognize God as Lord is to acknowledge that he is sovereign and supreme in the universe. To accept him as Savior is to accept his gift of salvation offered on the cross. To regard him as Father is to go a step further. Ideally, a father is the one in your life who provides and protects. This is exactly what God has done.

He has provided for your needs (Matthew 6:25–34). He has protected you from harm (Psalm 139:5). He has adopted you (Ephesians 1:5). And he has given you his name (1 John 3:1).

God has proven himself as a faithful Father. Now it falls to us to be trusting children.

He Still Moves Stones

We have nothing to offer you in exchange for what you have given us, Father. It's not that we don't have any value; it's just that we don't have any right to request the forgiveness we so desperately need and you are so willing to share. Your blessings amaze us.

Praise be to the God and Father of our Lord Jesus Christ. In Christ, God has given us every spiritual blessing in the heavenly world. That is, in Christ, he chose us before the world was made so that we would be his holy people—people without blame before him.
Ephesians 1:3–4

The same Lord is the Lord of all and gives many blessings to all who trust in him, as the Scripture says, "Anyone who calls on the Lord will be saved."
Romans 10:12–13

Every good action and every perfect gift is from God. These good gifts come down from the Creator of the sun, moon, and stars, who does not change like their shifting shadows.
James 1:17

GOD'S GUIDANCE

You've been there. You've escaped the sandy foundations of the valley and ascended his grand out-cropping of granite. You've turned your back on the noise and sought his voice. You've stepped away from the masses and followed the Master as he led you up the winding path to the summit.

Gently your guide invites you to sit on the rock above the tree line and look out with him at the ancient peaks that will never erode. "What is necessary is still what is sure," he confides. "Just remember:

"You'll go nowhere tomorrow that I haven't already been.

"Truth will still triumph.

"The victory is yours."

The sacred summit. A place of permanence in a world of transition.

The Applause of Heaven

Father, we invite you to be our guide through life. We surrender our lives to you. We welcome your holy guidance.

INSPIRATIONAL PROMISES

The LORD will always lead you. He will satisfy your needs in dry lands and give strength to your bones. You will be like a garden that has much water, like a spring that never runs dry.

Isaiah 58:11

People make plans in their minds, but only the LORD can make them come true. . . . Depend on the LORD in whatever you do, and your plans will succeed.

Proverbs 16:1, 3

Do not be shaped by this world; instead be changed within by a new way of thinking. Then you will be able to decide what God wants for you; you will know what is good and pleasing to him and what is perfect.

Romans 12:2

God's Grace

You may be decent. You may pay taxes and kiss your kids and sleep with a clean conscience. But apart from Christ you aren't holy. So how can you go to heaven?

Only believe. Accept the work already done, the work of Jesus on the cross.

Accept the goodness of Jesus Christ. Abandon your own works and accept his. Abandon your own decency and accept his. Stand before God in his name, not yours.

It's that easy? There was nothing easy about it at all. The cross was heavy, the blood was real, and the price was extravagant. It would have bankrupted you or me, so he paid it for us. Call it simple. Call it a gift. But don't call it easy.

Call it what it is. Call it grace.

A Gentle Thunder

Father, how holy and great is your promise. You've been so good to us. Help us to be busy about the right business—the business of serving you.

Our high priest is able to understand our weaknesses. When he lived on earth, he was tempted in every way that we are, but he did not sin. Let us, then, feel very sure that we can come before God's throne where there is grace. There we can receive mercy and grace to help us when we need it.

Hebrews 4:15–16

You have been saved by grace through believing. You did not save yourselves; it was a gift from God. It was not the result of your own efforts, so you cannot brag about it.

Ephesians 2:8–9

After you suffer for a short time, God, who gives all grace, will make everything right. He will make you strong and support you and keep you from falling. He called you to share in his glory in Christ, a glory that will continue forever.

1 Peter 5:10

GOD'S POWER

With one decision, history began. Existence became measurable.

Out of nothing came light.

Out of light came day.

Then came sky . . . and earth.

And on this earth? A mighty hand went to work.

Canyons were carved. Oceans were dug. Mountains erupted out of flatlands. Stars were flung. A universe sparkled.

Look to the canyons to see the Creator's splendor. Touch the flowers and see his delicacy. Listen to the thunder and hear his power. But gaze on [humanity]—the zenith—and witness all three . . . and more.

Today you will encounter God's creation. When you see the beauty around you, let each detail remind you to lift your head in praise. Express your appreciation for God's creation. Encourage others to see the beauty of his creation.

In the Eye of the Storm

Lord, we thank you and praise you for blessing us with such beautiful surroundings in which to live. May we never be so busy that we miss seeing your presence in all of your creation.

I praise your greatness, my God the King; I will praise you forever and ever. I will praise you every day; I will praise you forever and ever. The LORD is great and worthy of our praise; no one can understand how great he is.

Psalm 145:1–3

When the LORD All-Powerful makes a plan, no one can stop it. When the LORD raises his hand to punish people, no one can stop it.

Isaiah 14:27

I will announce the name of the LORD. Praise God because he is great! He is like a rock; what he does is perfect, and he is always fair. He is a faithful God who does no wrong, who is right and fair.

Deuteronomy 32:3–4

Inspirational
Promises About
Christian Living

SERVING GOD

On one side stands the crowd. Jeering. Baiting. Demanding.

On the other stands a peasant. Swollen lips. Lumpy eye. Lofty promise.

One promises acceptance, the other a cross.

One offers flesh and flash, the other offers faith.

The crowd challenges, "Follow us and fit in."

Jesus promises, "Follow me and stand out."

They promise to please.

God promises to save.

God looks at you and asks . . .

Which will be your choice?

A Gentle Thunder

Thank you, Lord, for offering us more than this world ever could. May we be spurred on by your love to do great works, yet never substitute those works for your great grace. Keep us amazed and mesmerized by what you have done for us.

In all the work you are doing, work the best you can. Work as if you were doing it for the Lord, not for people. Remember that you will receive your reward from the Lord, which he promised to his people. You are serving the Lord Christ.

Colossians 3:23–24

Then Jesus called the crowd to him, along with his followers. He said, "If people want to follow me, they must give up the things they want. They must be willing even to give up their lives to follow me. Those who want to save their lives will give up true life. But those who give up their lives for me and for the Good News will have true life."

Mark 8:34–35

"The servant does not get any special thanks for doing what his master commanded. It is the same with you. When you have done everything you are told to do, you should say, 'We are unworthy servants; we have only done the work we should do.'"

Luke 17:9–10

PRAISING GOD

Worship. In two thousand years we haven't worked out the kinks. We still struggle for the right words in prayer. We still fumble over Scripture. We don't know when to kneel. We don't know when to stand. We don't know how to pray.

Worship is a daunting task.

For that reason, God gave us the Psalms—a praise book for God's people. . . . This collection of hymns and petitions is strung together by one thread—a heart hungry for God.

Some are defiant. Others are reverent. Some are to be sung. Others are to be prayed. Some are intensely personal. Others are written as if the whole world would use them.

The very variety should remind us that worship is personal. No secret formula exists. What moves you may stymie another. Each worships differently. But each should worship.

The Inspirational Study Bible

We give you praise. We honor and glorify your name. You truly are the King of kings and the Lord of lords. You alone are worthy!

Praise the LORD for the glory of his name; worship the LORD because he is holy.

Psalm 29:2

Sing praises to the LORD, you who belong to him; praise his holy name.

Psalm 30:4

Come, let's worship him and bow down. Let's kneel before the LORD who made us, because he is our God and we are the people he takes care of, the sheep that he tends.

Psalm 95:6–7

Praise the LORD! Praise God in his Temple; praise him in his mighty heaven. Praise him for his strength; praise him for his greatness. . . . Let everything that breathes praise the LORD. Praise the LORD!

Psalm 150:1–2, 6

Giving to God

"Blessed are the meek," Jesus explained. Blessed are the available. Blessed are the conduits, the tunnels, the tools. Deliriously joyful are the ones who believe that if God has used sticks, rocks, and spit to do his will, then he can use us...

A small cathedral outside Bethlehem marks the supposed birthplace of Jesus. Behind a high altar in the church is a cave, a little cavern lit by silver lamps.

You can enter the main edifice and admire the ancient church. You can also enter the quiet cave where a star embedded in the floor recognizes the birth of the King. There is one stipulation, however. You have to stoop. The door is so low you can't go in standing up.

You can see the world standing tall, but to witness the Savior, you have to get on your knees.

The Applause of Heaven

Father, help us renew our commitment to you, to release everything and to be owned and possessed by you. We give ourselves completely to you—all that we are and all that we have.

Honor the LORD with your wealth and the firstfruits from all your crops. Then your barns will be full, and your wine barrels will overflow with new wine.

Proverbs 3:9–10

"Bring to the storehouse a full tenth of what you earn so there will be food in my house. Test me in this. . . . I will open the windows of heaven for you and pour out all the blessings you need."

Malachi 3:10

"Give, and you will receive. You will be given much. Pressed down, shaken together, and running over, it will spill into your lap. The way you give to others is the way God will give to you."

Luke 6:38

READING GOD'S WORD

The Bible has been banned, burned, scoffed, and ridiculed. Scholars have mocked it as foolish. Kings have branded it as illegal. A thousand times over, the grave has been dug and the dirge has begun, but somehow the Bible never stays in the grave. Not only has it survived; it has thrived. It is the single most popular book in all of history. It has been the best-selling book in the world for years!

There is no way on earth to explain it. Which perhaps is the only explanation. The answer? The Bible's durability is not found on earth; it is found in heaven. For the millions who have tested its claims and claimed its promises, there is but one answer—the Bible is God's book and God's voice.

The purpose of the Bible is to proclaim God's plan and passion to save his children.

That is the reason this book has endured through the centuries. . . . It is the treasure map that leads us to God's highest treasure, eternal life.

The Inspirational Study Bible

Father, we're amazed at how practical your Bible is. Help us to look for your guidance in that precious book.

God's word is alive and working and is sharper than a double-edged sword. It cuts all the way into us, where the soul and the spirit are joined, to the center of our joints and bones. And it judges the thoughts and feelings in our hearts.

Hebrews 4:12

The truly happy people are those who carefully study God's perfect law that makes people free, and they continue to study it. They do not forget what they heard, but they obey what God's teaching says. Those who do this will be made happy.

James 1:25

As newborn babies want milk, you should want the pure and simple teaching. By it you can mature in your salvation, because you have already examined and seen how good the Lord is.

1 Peter 2:2–3

OBEYING GOD

Compared to God's part, our part is minuscule but necessary. We don't have to do much, but we do have to do something.

Write a letter.
Ask forgiveness.
Call a counselor.
Confess.
Call mom.
Visit a doctor.
Be baptized.
Feed a hungry person.
Pray.
Teach.
Go.

Do something that demonstrates faith. For faith with no effort is no faith at all.

He Still Moves Stones

Father, your love compels us to do what we never thought we could do and go to heights we never thought we could reach. We step out in faith to be obedient to you!

"I have obeyed my Father's commands, and I remain in his love. In the same way, if you obey my commands, you will remain in my love. I have told you these things so that you can have the same joy I have and so that your joy will be the fullest possible joy."

John 15:10–11

"I will show you what everyone is like who comes to me and hears my words and obeys. That person is like a man building a house who dug deep and laid the foundation on rock. When the floods came, the water tried to wash the house away, but it could not shake it, because the house was built well."

Luke 6:47–48

We can be sure that we know God if we obey his commands. Anyone who says, "I know God," but does not obey God's commands is a liar, and the truth is not in that person. But if someone obeys God's teaching, then in that person God's love has truly reached its goal.

1 John 2:3–5

PRAYING TO GOD

What Jesus dreamed of doing and what he seemed able to do were separated by an impossible gulf. So Jesus prayed.

We don't know what he prayed about. But I have my guesses. . . . He prayed for the impossible to happen.

Or maybe I'm wrong. Maybe he didn't ask for anything. Maybe he just stood quietly in the presence of Presence and basked in the Majesty. Perhaps he placed his war-weary self before the throne and rested.

Maybe he lifted his head out of the confusion of earth long enough to hear the solution of heaven. Perhaps he was reminded that hard hearts don't faze the Father. That problem people don't perturb the Eternal One.

In the Eye of the Storm

Father, when you were on earth, you prayed. In your hours of distress, you retreated into moments of prayer. In your hours of joy, you lifted your heart and hands in prayer. Help us to be more like you in this way. Help us to make prayer a priority in our daily lives.

INSPIRATIONAL PROMISES

"So I tell you to believe that you have received the things you ask for in prayer, and God will give them to you. When you are praying, if you are angry with someone, forgive him so that your Father in heaven will also forgive your sins."

Mark 11:24–25

"If my people, who are called by my name, will humble themselves, if they will pray and seek me and stop their evil ways, I will hear them from heaven. I will forgive their sin, and I will heal their land."

2 Chronicles 7:14

*The L*ORD *sees the good people and listens to their prayers. But the L*ORD *is against those who do evil; he makes the world forget them.*

Psalm 34:15–16

LOVING GOD

He placed one scoop of clay upon another until a form lay lifeless on the ground.

All were silent as the Creator reached in himself and removed something yet unseen. "It's called 'choice.' The seed of choice."

Within the man, God had placed a divine seed. A seed of his self. The God of might had created earth's mightiest. The Creator had created, not a creature, but another creator. And the One who had chosen to love had created one who could love in return.

Now it's our choice.

In the Eye of the Storm

Father, we choose to love you. And we choose to reach out with your love to others who need you.

INSPIRATIONAL PROMISES

"If you love me, you will obey my commands. . . . Those who know my commands and obey them are the ones who love me, and my Father will love those who love me. I will love them and will show myself to them."

John 14:15, 21

"The most important command is this . . . 'Love the Lord your God with all your heart, all your soul, all your mind, and all your strength.'"

Mark 12:29–30

We love because God first loved us. . . . Those who do not love their brothers and sisters, whom they have seen, cannot love God, whom they have never seen. And God gave us this command: Those who love God must also love their brothers and sisters.

1 John 4:19–21

TRUSTING GOD

Many players appear on the stage of Gethsemane. Judas and his betrayal. Peter and his sword. . . . The soldiers and their weapons. And though these are crucial, they aren't instrumental. The encounter is not between Jesus and the soldiers; it is between God and Satan. Satan dares to enter yet another garden, but God stands and Satan hasn't a prayer.

Satan falls in the presence of Christ. One word from his lips, and the finest army in the world collapsed.

Satan is silent in the proclamation of Christ. Not once did the enemy speak without Jesus' invitation. Before Christ, Satan has nothing to say.

Satan is powerless against the protection of Christ.

When Jesus says he will keep you safe, he means it. Hell will have to get through him to get to you. Jesus is able to protect you. When he says he will get you home, he will get you home.

A Gentle Thunder

Father, help us today to remain faithful to you, even in times when we're surrounded by people who don't agree with us.

We worship God through his Spirit, and our pride is in Christ Jesus. We do not put trust in ourselves or anything we can do.

Philippians 3:3

"The person who trusts in the LORD will be blessed. The LORD will show him that he can be trusted. He will be strong, like a tree planted near water that sends its roots by a stream. It is not afraid when the days are hot; its leaves are always green. It does not worry in a year when no rain comes; it always produces fruit."

Jeremiah 17:7–8

When I am afraid, I will trust you. I praise God for his word. I trust God, so I am not afraid. What can human beings do to me?

Psalm 56:3–4

WORSHIPING GOD

Worship is the "thank you" that refuses to be silenced.

We have tried to make a science out of worship. We can't do that. We can't do that any more than we can "sell love" or "negotiate peace."

Worship is a voluntary act of gratitude offered by the saved to the Savior, by the healed to the Healer, and by the delivered to the Deliverer.

In the Eye of the Storm

We remember all that you have done for us, Father. We remember your goodness to us in the past. We remember your closeness in the present. We remember your power for the future. We worship you.

Respect the LORD your God. You must worship him and make your promises only in his name. Do not worship other gods as the people around you do, because the LORD your God is a jealous God.

Deuteronomy 6:13–15

Say to God, "Your works are amazing! Because your power is great, your enemies fall before you. All the earth worships you and sings praises to you. They sing praises to your name."

Psalm 66:3–4

"The time is coming when the true worshipers will worship the Father in spirit and truth, and that time is here already. You see, the Father too is actively seeking such people to worship him. God is spirit, and those who worship him must worship in spirit and truth."

John 4:23–24

Inspirational
Promises of
Guidance

WHEN YOU ARE TEMPTED

I stand a few feet from a mirror and see the face of a man who failed, . . . who failed his Maker. Again. I promised I wouldn't, but I did.

I was quiet when I should have been bold. I took a seat when I should have taken a stand.

If this were the first time, it would be different. But it isn't. How many times can one fall and expect to be caught?

Your eyes look in the mirror and see a sinner, a failure, a promise-breaker. But by faith you look in the mirror and see a robed prodigal bearing the ring of grace on your finger and the kiss of your Father on your face.

Your eyes see your faults. Your faith sees your Savior. Your eyes see your guilt. You faith sees his blood.

When God Whispers Your Name

Father, when we confront temptation, when we stand face-to-face with evil, we pray that you would give us strength and that you would use your power to block the path of evil.

So the Lord knows how to save those who serve him when troubles come.

2 Peter 2:9

Be strong in the Lord and in his great power. Put on the full armor of God so that you can fight against the devil's evil tricks. Our fight is not against people on earth but against the rulers and authorities and the powers of this world's darkness, against the spiritual powers of evil in the heavenly world.

Ephesians 6:10–12

If you think you are strong, you should be careful not to fall. The only temptation that has come to you is that which everyone has. But you can trust God, who will not permit you to be tempted more than you can stand. But when you are tempted, he will also give you a way to escape so that you will be able to stand it.

1 Corinthians 10:12–13

WHEN YOU FEEL GUILTY

Have you been there? Have you felt the ground of conviction give way beneath your feet? The ledge crumbles, your eyes widen, and down you go. Poof!

Now what do you do? . . . When we fall, we can dismiss it. We can deny it. We can distort it. Or we can deal with it.

We keep no secrets from God. Confession is not telling God what we did. He already knows. Confession is simply agreeing with God that our acts were wrong.

How can God heal what we deny? . . . How can God grant us pardon when we won't admit our guilt?

Ahh, there's that word: guilt. Isn't that what we avoid? Guilt. Isn't that what we detest? But is guilt so bad? What does guilt imply if not that we know right from wrong, that we aspire to be better than we are. . . . That's what guilt is: a healthy regret for telling God one thing and doing another.

A Gentle Thunder

We are not perfect, Father, but we are yours. We're not what we should be, but we do claim your salvation and your grace. Thank you for the immeasurable depth of your grace.

*If anyone belongs to Christ, there is a new creation.
The old things have gone; everything is made new!*

2 Corinthians 5:17

*So now, those who are in Christ Jesus are not judged
guilty.*

Romans 8:1

*When you were spiritually dead because of your sins
and because you were not free from the power of your
sinful self, God made you alive with Christ, and he
forgave all our sins. He canceled the debt, which listed
all the rules we failed to follow. He took away that
record with its rules and nailed it to the cross.*

Colossians 2:13–14

*"I, I am the One who forgives all your sins, for my
sake; I will not remember your sins."*

Isaiah 43:25

WHEN YOU WORRY

Worry . . . makes you forget who's in charge.

And when the focus is on yourself . . . you worry. You become anxious about many things. You worry that:

Your co-workers won't appreciate you.

Your leaders will overwork you.

Your superintendent won't understand you.

Your congregation won't support you.

With time, your agenda becomes more important than God's. You're more concerned with presenting self than pleasing him. And you may even find yourself doubting God's judgment.

God has gifted you with talents. He has done the same to your neighbor. If you concern yourself with your neighbor's talents, you will neglect yours. But if you concern yourself with yours, you could inspire both.

He Still Moves Stones

Lord, we don't ask that you take from us the worries of this life but that you reveal the worries of this life so that we can share them with you and turn them over to you.

Give all your worries to [God], because he cares about you.

1 Peter 5:7

Jesus said, "Don't let your hearts be troubled. Trust in God, and trust in me."

John 14:1

You, LORD, give true peace to those who depend on you, because they trust you. So, trust the LORD always, because he is our Rock forever.

Isaiah 26:3–4

When You Suffer

There is a window in your heart through which you can see God. Once upon a time that window was clear. Your view of God was crisp. You could see God as vividly as you could see a gentle valley or hillside.

Then, suddenly, the window cracked. A pebble broke the window. A pebble of pain.

And suddenly God was not so easy to see. The view that had been so crisp had changed.

You were puzzled. God wouldn't allow something like this to happen, would he?

When you can't see him, trust him. . . . Jesus is closer than you've ever dreamed.

In the Eye of the Storm

Father, we believe that when we see you, any suffering that we endured on the face of this earth will be worth it. Help us to understand your sovereign ways. And when we cannot understand, help us to trust.

Those who go to God Most High for safety will be protected by the Almighty. I will say to the LORD, "You are my place of safety and protection. You are my God and I trust you."

Psalm 91:1–2

LORD, even when I have trouble all around me, you will keep me alive. When my enemies are angry, you will reach down and save me by your power.

Psalm 138:7

"I leave you peace; my peace I give you. I do not give it to you as the world does. So don't let your hearts be troubled or afraid."

John 14:27

WHEN YOU HAVE DOUBTS

Thomas came with doubts. Did Christ turn him away?

Moses had his reservations. Did God tell him to go home?

Job had his struggles. Did God avoid him?

Paul had his hard times. Did God abandon him?

No. God never turns away the sincere heart. Tough questions don't stump God. He invites our probing.

Mark it down. God never turns away the honest seeker. Go to God with your questions. You may not find all the answers, but in finding God, you know the One who does.

Walking with the Savior

We pray, O Father, that in the hours when we find ourselves in the dungeons of doubt, you will hear our questions. Forgive us for demanding that you answer our questions as we want them answered. Decrease our doubt; increase our faith.

Inspirational Promises

If any of you needs wisdom, you should ask God for it. He is generous to everyone and will give you wisdom without criticizing you.

James 1:5

May God himself, the God of peace, make you pure, belonging only to him. May your whole self—spirit, soul, and body—be kept safe and without fault when our Lord Jesus Christ comes.

1 Thessalonians 5:23

The ways of God are without fault. The LORD's words are pure. He is a shield to those who trust him. Who is God? Only the LORD. Who is the Rock? Only our God.

Psalm 18:30–31

WHEN YOU ARE ANGRY

Anger. It's easy to define: the noise of the soul. Anger. The unseen irritant of the heart. Anger. The relentless invader of silence.

The louder it gets, the more desperate we become.

Some of you are thinking . . . *You don't have any idea how hard my life has been.* And you're right, I don't. But I have a very clear idea how miserable your future will be unless you deal with your anger.

X-ray the world of the vengeful and behold the tumor of bitterness: black, menacing, malignant. Carcinoma of the spirit. Its fatal fibers creep around the edge of the heart and ravage it. Yesterday you can't alter, but your reaction to yesterday you can. The past you cannot change, but your response to your past you can.

When God Whispers Your Name

Father, at one time or another we have all looked at the circumstances of our lives and wondered why certain things happen. Yet your Word gives great encouragement from others who sought you in their own time of need, and found you. You have been faithful in the past, and you are faithful now to bring peace and calm in any circumstance.

The wisdom that comes from God is first of all pure, then peaceful, gentle, and easy to please. This wisdom is always ready to help those who are troubled and to do good for others. It is always fair and honest.

James 3:17

When you are angry, do not sin, and be sure to stop being angry before the end of the day. Do not give the devil a way to defeat you.

Ephesians 4:26–27

My dear brothers and sisters, always be willing to listen and slow to speak. Do not become angry easily, because anger will not help you live the right kind of life God wants.

James 1:19–20

WHEN YOU ARE
DISCOURAGED

Is there anything more frail than a bruised reed? Look at the bruised reed at the water's edge. A once slender and tall stalk of sturdy river grass, it is now bowed and bent.

Are you a bruised reed? Was it so long ago that you stood so tall, so proud?

Then something happened. You were bruised . . .

by harsh words
by a friend's anger
by a spouse's betrayal
by your own failure
by religion's rigidity.

Painted on canvas after canvas is the tender touch of a Creator who has a special place for the bruised and weary of the world.

He Still Moves Stones

Thank you, Father, that when we are bruised, we are not left to wilt and die. Your comfort, healing, and restoration are an ever-present wellspring of help and reassurance of your love.

Inspirational Promises

Do not lose the courage you had in the past, which has a great reward. You must hold on, so you can do what God wants and receive what he has promised.

Hebrews 10:35–36

We must not become tired of doing good. We will receive our harvest of eternal life at the right time if we do not give up.

Galatians 6:9

God began doing a good work in you, and I am sure he will continue it until it is finished when Jesus Christ comes again.

Philippians 1:6

Lord, even when I have trouble all around me, you will keep me alive. When my enemies are angry, you will reach down and save me by your power.

Psalm 138:7

Inspirational Promises About Personal Relationships

RESTORING BROKEN RELATIONSHIPS

Jesus described for his followers what he came to do. He came to build a relationship with people. He came to take away the enmity, to take away the strife, to take away the isolation that existed between God and man. Once he bridged that, once he overcame that, he said, "I call you friends."

In repairing a relationship, it's essential to realize that no friendship is perfect, no marriage is perfect, no person is perfect. With the resolve that you are going to make a relationship work, you can develop peace treaties of love and tolerance and harmony to transform a difficult situation into something beautiful.

Walking with the Savior

Father, take that which is broken in our relationships and bless it with your healing power of restoration. And create in us a renewed sense of commitment to each other as well as make every effort to continue together in this way.

Inspirational Promises

I urge you who have been chosen by God to live up to the life to which God called you. Always be humble, gentle, and patient, accepting each other in love. You are joined together with peace through the Spirit, so make every effort to continue together in this way.

Ephesians 4:1–3

Love each other deeply, because love will cause people to forgive each other for many sins. Open your homes to each other, without complaining. Each of you has received a gift to use to serve others. Be good servants of God's various gifts of grace.

1 Peter 4:8–10

Be sure that no one pays back wrong for wrong, but always try to do what is good for each other and for all people.

1 Thessalonians 5:15

RESOLVING RESENTMENT

Resentment is the cocaine of the emotions. It causes our blood to pump and our energy level to rise. But, also like cocaine, it demands increasingly large and more frequent dosages. There is a dangerous point at which anger ceases to be an emotion and becomes a driving force. A person bent on revenge moves unknowingly further and further away from being able to forgive, for to be without the anger is to be without a source of energy.

Hatred is the rabid dog that turns on its owner.

Revenge is the raging fire that consumes the arsonist.

Bitterness is the trap that snares the hunter.

And mercy is the choice that can set them all free.

The Applause of Heaven

Father, we know that resentment and bitterness don't belong in Christian hearts. Help us turn our toxic feelings over to you, Father. Remind us that your touch can turn brokenness into strength.

So why do you judge your brothers or sisters in Christ? And why do you think you are better than they are? We will all stand before God to be judged.

Romans 14:10

The Lord hates evil thoughts but is pleased with kind words.

Proverbs 15:26

Whoever forgives someone's sin makes a friend, but gossiping about the sin breaks up friendships.

Proverbs 17:9

All of you should be in agreement, understanding each other, loving each other as family, being kind and humble. Do not do wrong to repay a wrong, and do not insult to repay an insult. But repay with a blessing, because you yourselves were called to do this so that you might receive a blessing.

1 Peter 3:8–9

Praying for Others

Prayer is the recognition that if God had not engaged himself in our problems, we would still be lost in the blackness. It is by his mercy that we have been lifted up. Prayer is that whole process that reminds us of who God is and who we are.

I believe there's great power in prayer. I believe God heals the wounded, and that he can raise the dead. But I don't believe we tell God what to do and when to do it.

God knows that we, with our limited vision, don't even know that for which we should pray. When we entrust our requests to him, we trust him to honor our prayers with holy judgment.

Walking with the Savior

Father, it is an honor to be able to open our hearts to you in prayer. No matter the time or the place, you hear our cries, and we are truly thankful. Help us to be always mindful of praying for others in their time of need, and praying with others as we live for your glory.

INSPIRATIONAL PROMISES

"I tell you that if two of you on earth agree about something and pray for it, it will be done for you by my Father in heaven. This is true because if two or three people come together in my name, I am there with them."

Matthew 18:19–20

Confess your sins to each other and pray for each other so God can heal you. When a believing person prays, great things happen.

James 5:16

"Do good to those who hate you, bless those who curse you, pray for those who are cruel to you."

Luke 6:27–28

Brothers and sisters, I beg you to help me in my work by praying to God for me. Do this because of our Lord Jesus and the love that the Holy Spirit gives us.

Romans 15:30

COPING WITH CONFLICT

Want to see a miracle? Plant a word of love heart-deep in a person's life. Nurture it with a smile and a prayer, and watch what happens.

An employee gets a compliment. A wife receives a bouquet of flowers.

Sowing seeds of peace is like sowing beans. You don't know why it works; you just know it does. Seeds are planted, and topsoils of hurt are shoved away.

Jesus modeled this. We don't see him settling many disputes or negotiating conflicts. But we do see him cultivating inward harmony through acts of love.

He built bridges by healing hurts. He prevented conflict by touching the interior. He cultivated harmony by sowing seeds of peace in fertile hearts.

The Applause of Heaven

God of peace, teach us what it means to be peacemakers. Help us cultivate peace between others and you—in our neighborhoods, offices, schoolrooms. Teach us the art of building bridges and not walls.

If someone does wrong to you, do not pay him back by doing wrong to him. Try to do what everyone thinks is right. Do your best to live in peace with everyone.

Romans 12:17–18

"They are blessed who work for peace, for they will be called God's children."

Matthew 5:9

Agree with each other, and live in peace. Then the God of love and peace will be with you.

2 Corinthians 13:11

Being a Godly Parent

Never underestimate the ponderings of a Christian parent. Never underestimate the power that comes when a parent pleads with God on behalf of a child. Who knows how many prayers are being answered right now because of the faithful ponderings of a parent ten or twenty years ago? God listens to thoughtful parents.

Praying for our children is a noble task. If what we are doing, in this fast-paced society, is taking us away from prayer time for our children, we're doing too much. There is nothing more special, more precious, than time that a parent spends struggling and pondering with God on behalf of a child.

Walking with the Savior

Father, no matter how hectic our day or full our schedule, may we consistently make time to pray for our children, that their hearts would be guarded from this world, and their desires would be to follow you.

Inspirational Promises

Know and believe today that the LORD is God. He is God in heaven above and on the earth below. There is no other god! Obey his laws and commands that I am giving you today so that things will go well for you and your children. Then you will live a long time in the land that the LORD your God is giving to you forever.

Deuteronomy 4:39–40

Correct your children, and you will be proud; they will give you satisfaction.

Proverbs 29:17

All your children will be taught by the LORD, and they will have much peace.

Isaiah 54:13

Fathers, do not make your children angry, but raise them with the training and teaching of the Lord.

Ephesians 6:4

Valuing Others

God sees us with the eyes of a Father. He sees our defects, errors, and blemishes. But he also sees our value.

What did Jesus know that enabled him to do what he did?

Here's part of the answer. He knew the value of people. He knew that each human being is a treasure. And because he did, people were not a source of stress but a source of joy.

In the Eye of the Storm

Lord, thank you that, in spite our sin and weakness, you see something beautiful, something of value. In the same way, help us to see others with your eyes so that we may be a source of your unconditional love for them.

Inspirational Promises

My brothers and sisters, God called you to be free,
but do not use your freedom as an excuse to do what
pleases your sinful self. Serve each other with love. The
whole law is made complete in this one command:
"Love your neighbor as you love yourself."

Galatians 5:13–14

Let us think about each other and help each other to
show love and do good deeds.

Hebrews 10:24

In the same way, younger people should be willing to
be under older people. And all of you should be very
humble with each other. "God is against the proud, but
he gives grace to the humble."

1 Peter 5:5

SERVING OTHERS

There are times when we . . . are called to love, expecting nothing in return. Times when we are called to give money to people who will never say thanks, to forgive those who won't forgive us, to come early and stay late when no one else notices.

Service prompted by duty. This is the call of discipleship.

Mary and Mary knew a task had to be done—Jesus' body had to be prepared for burial. Peter didn't offer to do it. Andrew didn't volunteer. . . . So the two Marys decide to do it.

Mary and Mary thought they were alone. They weren't. They thought their journey was unnoticed. They were wrong. God knew. He was watching them walk up the mountain. He was measuring their steps. He was smiling at their hearts and thrilled at their devotion.

He Still Moves Stones

Lift up our eyes, Father, that we might see our world as you see it. Help us respond as you respond to the hurts around us.

If there are poor among you, in one of the towns of the land the LORD your God is giving you, do not be selfish or greedy toward them. But give freely to them, and freely lend them whatever they need.

Deuteronomy 15:7–8

Religion that God the father accepts as pure and without fault is this: caring for orphans or widows who need help, and keeping yourself free from the world's evil influence.

James 1:27

A brother or sister in Christ might need clothes or food. If you say to that person, "God be with you! I hope you stay warm and get plenty to eat," but you do not give what that person needs, your words are worth nothing.

James 2:15–16

Forgiving Others

Bitterness is its own prison.

The sides are slippery with resentment. A floor of muddy anger stills the feet. The stench of betrayal fills the air and stings the eyes. A cloud of self-pity blocks the view of the tiny exit above.

Step in and look at the prisoners. Victims are chained to the walls. Victims of betrayal. Victims of abuse.

The dungeon, deep and dark, is beckoning you to enter. . . . You can, you know. You've experienced enough hurt.

You can choose, like many, to chain yourself to your hurt. . . . Or you can choose, like some, to put away your hurts before they become hates.

How does God deal with your bitter heart? He reminds you that what you have is more important than what you don't have. You still have your relationship with God. No one can take that.

He Still Moves Stones

Father, sometimes forgiving others seems impossible. Remind us that revisiting the cross is the first step in knowing how to forgive.

Inspirational Promises

"When you are praying, if you are angry with someone, forgive him so that your Father in heaven will also forgive your sins."

Mark 11:25

God has chosen you and made you his holy people. He loves you. So you should always clothe yourselves with mercy, kindness, humility, gentleness, and patience. Bear with each other, and forgive each other. If someone does wrong to you, forgive that person because the Lord forgave you.

Colossians 3:12–13

Be kind and loving to each other, and forgive each other just as God forgave you in Christ.

Ephesians 4:32

Being Hospitable

Here's a suggestion: We should all wear antennae to work, to church, to school—antennae that pick up on people who seem out of place, whose loneliness shows. We should be the ones to approach these folks and extend friendship to them. Maybe you think the last thing you need is another friend. But friendliness—hospitality—is a virtue that brings as much joy to the giver as to the receiver.

When you extend hospitality to others, you're not trying to impress people, you're trying to reflect God to them.

Walking with the Savior

Father, open our eyes and hearts to those around us who need a friend. And give us the courage to step out of our comfort zones to reach out to them in your name.

Inspirational Promises

"Then the King will say to the people on his right, 'Come, my Father has given you his blessing. Receive the kingdom God has prepared for you since the world was made. I was hungry, and you gave me food. I was thirsty, and you gave me something to drink. I was alone and away from home, and you invited me into your house. I was without clothes, and you gave me something to wear. I was sick, and you cared for me. I was in prison, and you visited me.'"

Matthew 25:34–36

"Those who give one of these little ones a cup of cold water because they are my followers will truly get their reward."

Matthew 10:42

Remember to welcome strangers, because some who have done this have welcomed angels without knowing it. Remember those who are in prison as if you were in prison with them. Remember those who are suffering as if you were suffering with them.

Hebrews 13:2–3

Having Compassion

Picture a battleground strewn with wounded bodies, and you see Bethesda. Imagine a nursing home overcrowded and understaffed, and you see the pool. Call to mind the orphans in Bangladesh or the abandoned in New Delhi, and you will see what people saw when they passed Bethesda. As they passed, what did they hear? An endless wave of groans. What did they witness? A field of faceless need. What did they do? Most walked past, ignoring the people.

But not Jesus.

He is alone. . . . The people need him—so he's there. Can you picture it? Jesus walking among the suffering.

Little do they know that God is walking slowly, stepping carefully between the beggars and the blind.

He Still Moves Stones

Lord, give us the compassion and courage to walk toward the hurting instead of away. Create in us the conviction to embrace the downtrodden so that we can be even a small glimmer of encouragement and comfort. And may we do this in the spirit of your love.

Inspirational Promises

If you have any encouragement from being united with Christ, if any comfort from his love, if any fellowship with the Spirit, if any tenderness and compassion, then make my joy complete by being like-minded, having the same love, being one in spirit and purpose. Do nothing out of selfish ambition or vain conceit, but in humility consider others better than yourselves.

Philippians 2:1–3 NIV

By helping each other with your troubles, you truly obey the law of Christ.

Galatians 6:2

This is how we know what real love is: Jesus gave his life for us. So we should give our lives for our brothers and sisters. Suppose someone has enough to live and sees a brother or sister in need, but does not help. Then God's love is not living in that person. My children, we should love people not only with words and talk, but by our actions and true caring.

1 John 3:16–18

Inspirational Promises of Wisdom

DEVELOPING A SENSE OF SELF-WORTH

"He made perfect forever those who are being made holy."

Underline the word *perfect*. Note that the word is not *better*. Not *improving*. Not *on the upswing*. God doesn't improve; he perfects. He doesn't enhance; he completes.

Now, I realize that there's a sense in which we're imperfect. We still err. We still stumble. We still do exactly what we don't want to do. And that part of us is, according to the verse, "being made holy."

But when it comes to our position before God, we're perfect. When he sees each of us, he sees one who has been made perfect through the One who is perfect—Jesus Christ.

In the Eye of the Storm

We thank you, Father, that you see and care for each one of your children. We thank you that we are all equally valuable to you. Remind us of the your love when we feel lost among the crowd.

INSPIRATIONAL PROMISES

People should think of us as servants of Christ, the ones God has trusted with his secrets. Now in this way those who are trusted with something valuable must show they are worthy of that trust. As for myself, I do not care if I am judged by you or by any human court. I do not even judge myself. . . . The Lord is the One who judges me.

1 Corinthians 4:1–4

Do not let anyone treat you as if you are unimportant because you are young. Instead, be an example to the believers with your words, your actions, your love, your faith, and your pure life.

1 Timothy 4:12

You have begun to live the new life, in which you are being made new and are becoming like the One who made you. This new life brings you the true knowledge of God. In the new life there is no difference between Greeks and Jews. . . . There is no difference between slaves and free people. But Christ is in all believers, and Christ is all that is important.

Colossians 3:10–11

REPENTING OF WRONG

No one is happier than the one who has sincerely repented of wrong. Repentance is the decision to turn from selfish desires and seek God. It is a genuine, sincere regret that creates sorrow and moves us to admit wrong and to desire to do better.

It's an inward conviction that expresses itself in outward actions.

You look at the love of God and you can't believe he's loved you like he has, and this realization motivates you to change your life. That is the nature of repentance.

Walking with the Savior

Blessed Lord, give us the conviction and the courage to repent when we have sinned. Help us to remember that the blessing is all ours when we do, for you are a God of mercy and love. It is because of you, we are forgiven!

Inspirational Promises

The Lord is not slow in doing what he promised—the way some people understand slowness. But God is being patient with you. He does not want anyone to be lost, but he wants all people to change their hearts and lives.

2 Peter 3:9

[God] has been very kind and patient, waiting for you to change, but you think nothing of his kindness. Perhaps you do not understand that God is kind to you so you will change your hearts and lives.

Romans 2:4

Whoever accepts correction is on the way to life, but whoever ignores correction will lead others away from life.

Proverbs 10:17

FINDING REST

Time has skyrocketed in value. The value of any commmodity depends on its scarcity. And time that once was abundant now is going to the highest bidder.

When I was ten years old, my mother enrolled me in piano lessons. . . . Spending thirty minutes every afternoon tethered to a piano bench was a torture just one level away from swallowing broken glass.

Some of the music, though, I learned to enjoy. I hammered the staccatos. I belabored the crescendos. . . . But there was one instruction in the music I could never obey to my teacher's satisfaction. The rest. The zigzagged command to do nothing. What sense does that make? Why sit at the piano and pause when you can pound?

"Because," my teacher patiently explained, "music is always sweeter after a rest."

It didn't make sense to me at age ten. But now, a few decades later, the words ring with wisdom—divine wisdom.

The Applause of Heaven

Father, let us never forget that our lives are sweeter when we rest in you.

"Remember to keep the Sabbath holy. Work and get everything done during six days each week, but the seventh day is a day of rest to honor the LORD your God. On that day no one may do any work. . . . The reason is that in six days the LORD made everything— the sky, the earth, the sea, and everything in them. On the seventh day he rested. So the LORD blessed the Sabbath day and made it holy."

Exodus 20:8–11

God will do what is right. He will give trouble to those who trouble you. And he will give rest to you who are troubled.

2 Thessalonians 1:6–7

We who have believed are able to enter and have God's rest.

Hebrews 4:3

SETTING PRIORITIES

There is only so much sand in the hourglass. Who gets it?

You know what I'm talking about, don't you?

"The PTA needs a new treasurer. With your background and experience and talent and wisdom and love for kids and degree in accounting, YOU are the perfect one for the job!"

It's tug-of-war, and you are the rope.

"Blessed are the meek," Jesus said. The word *meek* does not mean weak. It means focused. It is a word used to describe a domesticated stallion. Power under control. Strength with a direction.

Blessed are those who recognize their God-given responsibilities. Blessed are those who acknowledge that there is only one God and have quit applying for his position. Blessed are those who know what on earth they are on earth to do and set themselves about the business of doing it.

In the Eye of the Storm

Father, help us to say no to the world and yes to you. Help us to hear the true voice of Jesus Christ amid the voices of pressure and success and power.

Respecting the LORD and not being proud will bring you wealth, honor, and life.

Proverbs 22:4

In every way be an example of doing good deeds. When you teach, do it with honesty and seriousness. Speak the truth so that you cannot be criticized. . . . [Grace] teaches us to live in the present age in a wise and right way and in a way that shows we serve God. We should live like that while we wait for our great hope and the coming of the glory of our great God and Savior Jesus Christ.

Titus 2:7–8, 12–13

God is fair; he will not forget the work you did and the love you showed for him by helping his people. And he will remember that you are still helping them. We want each of you to go on with the same hard work all your lives so you will surely get what you hope for.

Hebrews 6:10–11

CORRECTING MISTAKES

Do-it-yourself Christianity is not much encouragement to the done in and worn out.

Self-sanctification holds little hope for the addict.

At some point we need more than good advice; we need help. Somewhere on this journey home, we realize that a fifty-fifty proposition is too little. We need more.

We need help. Help from the inside out. . . . Not near us. Not above us. Not around us. But in us. In the part of us we don't even know. In the heart no one else has seen. In the hidden recesses of our being dwells, not an angel, not a philosophy, not a genie, but God.

When God Whispers Your Name

Father, take our mistakes and turn them into opportunities. You have done this over and over in the lives of people like David, Paul, and Peter. We know you can do the same for us.

If you hide your sins, you will not succeed. If you confess and reject them, you will receive mercy.

Proverbs 28:13

If you listen to correction to improve your life, you will live among the wise. Those who refuse correction hate themselves, but those who accept correction gain understanding. Respect for the Lord will teach you wisdom. If you want to be honored, you must be humble.

Proverbs 15:31–33

In the kingdom of God . . . the important things are living right with God, peace, and joy in the Holy Spirit. Anyone who serves Christ by living this way is pleasing God and will be accepted by other people. So let us try to do what makes peace and helps one another.

Romans 14:17–19

FACING DISAPPOINTMENT

When God doesn't do what we want, it's not easy. Never has been. Never will be. But faith is the conviction that God knows more than we do about this life and he will get us through it.

Remember, disappointment is caused by unmet expectations. Disappointment is cured by revamped expectations.

Next time you're disappointed, don't panic. Don't give up. Just be patient and let God remind you he's still in control. It ain't over till it's over.

He Still Moves Stones

Father, we are thankful that you are in control of all life's situations. When we are disappointed, help us to turn to you and accept your will, confident that you always have our best interests at heart.

"*They are blessed who grieve, for God will comfort them. . . . They are blessed who hunger and thirst after justice, for they will be satisfied.*"

Matthew 5:4, 6

I pray that the God who gives hope will fill you with much joy and peace while you trust in him. Then your hope will overflow by the power of the Holy Spirit.

Romans 15:13

The LORD says, "My thoughts are not like your thoughts. Your ways are not like my ways. Just as the heavens are higher than the earth, so are my ways higher than your ways and my thoughts higher than your thoughts. . . . So you will go out with joy and be led out in peace."

Isaiah 55:8–9, 12

DEALING WITH THE PAST

Perhaps your childhood memories bring more hurt than inspiration. The voices of your past cursed you, belittled you, ignored you. At the time, you thought such treatment was typical. Now you see it isn't.

And now you find yourself trying to explain your past. Do you rise above the past and make a difference? Or do you remain controlled by the past and make excuses?

Think about this. Spiritual life comes from the Spirit! Your parents may have given you genes, but God gives you grace. Your parents may be responsible for your body, but God has taken charge of your soul. You may get your looks from your mother, but you get eternity from your Father, your heavenly Father. And God is willing to give you what your family didn't.

When God Whispers Your Name

Father, thank you that no matter what our past was like, we have strength, power, and hope in our future with you.

We know that in everything God works for the good of those who love him. They are the people he called, because that was his plan.

Romans 8:28

Why am I so sad? Why am I so upset? I should put my hope in God and keep praising him, my Savior and my God.

Psalm 43:5

I know that I have not yet reached that goal, but there is one thing I always do. Forgetting the past and straining toward what is ahead, I keep trying to reach the goal and get the prize for which God called me through Christ to the life above.

Philippians 3:13–14

Accepting God's Freedom

Jesus spoke of freedom, but he spoke of a different kind of freedom: the type of freedom that comes not through power but through submission. Not through control but through surrender. Not through possessions but through open hands.

God wants to emancipate his people; he wants to set them free. He wants his people to be not slaves but sons. He wants them governed not by law but by love.

We have been liberated from our own guilt and our own legalism. We have the freedom to pray and the freedom to love the God of our heart. And we have been forgiven by the only one who could condemn us. We are truly free!

Walking with the Savior

Father, thank you for the freedom we experience when we give our lives to you—freedom from guilt, from the world's standards, and from spending eternity other than in heaven with you. To you be all the glory.

In Christ we are set free by the blood of his death, and so we have forgiveness of sins.

Ephesians 1:7

"I tell you the truth, everyone who lives in sin is a slave to sin. A slave does not stay with a family forever, but a son belongs to the family forever. So if the Son makes you free, you will be truly free."

John 8:34–36

We have freedom now, because Christ made us free. So stand strong. Do not change and go back into the slavery of the law.

Galatians 5:1

MAKING THE RIGHT CHOICES

I have something against the lying voices that noise our world. You've heard them. They tell you to swap your integrity for a new sale. To barter your convictions for an easy deal. To exchange your devotion for a quick thrill.

They whisper. They woo. They taunt. They tantalize. They flirt. They flatter. "Go ahead, it's OK." "Don't worry, no one will know."

The world rams at your door; Jesus taps at your door. The voices scream for your allegiance; Jesus softly and tenderly requests it. The world promises flashy pleasure; Jesus promises a quiet dinner . . . with God.

Which voice do you hear?

In the Eye of the Storm

Lord, we want to hear from you! We want to know what you have to say. Help us to be still and hear your voice through all the noise and distraction in this world.

Trust the Lord with all your heart, and don't depend on your own understanding. Remember the Lord in all you do, and he will give you success.

Proverbs 3:5–6

You were taught to leave your old self—to stop living the evil way you lived before. That old self becomes worse, because people are fooled by the evil things they want to do. But you were taught to be made new in your hearts, to become a new person. That new person is made to be like God—made to be truly good and holy.

Ephesians 4:22–24

Now that you are obedient children of God do not live as you did in the past. You did not understand, so you did the evil things you wanted. But be holy in all you do, just as God, the One who called you, is holy.

1 Peter 1:14–15

Inspirational
Promises
About Jesus

Jesus, the Savior

He looked around the hill and foresaw a scene. Three figures hung on three crosses. Arms spread. Heads fallen forward. They moaned with the wind.

Men clad in soldiers' garb sat on the ground near the trio.

Men clad in religion stood off to one side. . . . Arrogant, cocky.

Women clad in sorrow huddled at the foot of the hill. . . . Faces tear streaked.

All heaven stood to fight. All nature rose to rescue. All eternity poised to protect. But the Creator gave no command.

"It must be done . . . ," he said, and withdrew.

The angel spoke again. "It would be less painful . . ."

The Creator interrupted softly. "But it wouldn't be love."

In the Eye of the Storm

Thank you, Father, for the message of Christ's life—a message of hope, a message of mercy, a message of light in a dark world. Thank you that because of his life and death we can receive salvation and eternal life.

Inspirational Promises

"God loved the world so much that he gave his one and only Son so that whoever believes in him may not be lost, but have eternal life. God did not send his Son into the world to judge the world guilty, but to save the world through him."

John 3:16–17

If you declare with your mouth, "Jesus is Lord," and if you believe in your heart that God raised Jesus from the dead, you will be saved.

Romans 10:9

We have seen and can testify that the Father sent his Son to be the Savior of the world.

1 John 4:14

JESUS, OUR LORD

Do you wonder where you can go for encouragement and motivation? Go back to that moment when you first saw the love of Jesus Christ. Remember the day when you were separated from Christ? You knew only guilt and confusion and then—a light. Someone opened a door and light came into your darkness, and you said in your heart, "I am redeemed!"

Run to Jesus. Jesus wants you to go to him. He wants to become the most important person in your life, the greatest love you'll ever know. He wants you to love him so much that there's no room in your heart and in your life for sin. Invite him to take up residence in your heart.

Walking with the Savior

Lord, thank you that we can run into your open arms at any time, and know that you will embrace us with your great love. We praise you and give you glory for your promise of redemption and everlasting life with you.

So God raised [Jesus] to the highest place. God made his name greater than every other name so that every knee will bow to the name of Jesus—everyone in heaven, on earth, and under the earth. And everyone will confess that Jesus Christ is Lord and bring glory to God the Father.

Philippians 2:9–11

We do not live or die for ourselves. If we live, we are living for the Lord, and if we die, we are dying for the Lord. So living or dying, we belong to the Lord.

Romans 14:7–8

The payment for sin is death. But God gives us a free gift of life forever in Christ Jesus our Lord.

Romans 6:23

Jesus Is Risen

The fire that lit the boiler of the New Testament church was an unquenchable belief that if Jesus had been only a man, he would have stayed in the tomb. The earliest Christians couldn't stay silent about the fact that the one they saw hung on a cross walked again on the earth and appeared to five hundred people.

Let us ask our Father humbly, yet confidently in the name of Jesus, to remind us of the empty tomb. Let us see the victorious Jesus: the conqueror of the tomb, the one who defied death. And let us be reminded that we, too, will be granted that same victory!

Walking with the Savior

Lord, thank you for the sweet surprise of Easter morning. We are thankful that when you arose from your sleep of death, you didn't go immediately to heaven, but instead you went and visited people. This visit of love reminds us that it was for people that you died.

Jesus said to [Martha], "I am the resurrection and the life. Those who believe in me will have life even if they die. And everyone who lives and believes in me will never die."

John 11:25–26

But Christ has truly been raised from the dead—the first one and proof that those who sleep in death will also be raised.

1 Corinthians 15:20

God raised the Lord Jesus from the dead, and we know that God will also raise us with Jesus. God will bring us together with you, and we will stand before him.

2 Corinthians 4:14

We believe that Jesus died and that he rose again. So, because of him, God will raise with Jesus those who have died.

1 Thessalonians 4:14

JESUS CARES FOR US

The shepherd knows his sheep. He calls them by name.

When we see a crowd, we see exactly that, a crowd.... We see people, not persons, but people. A herd of humans. A flock of faces. That's what we see.

But not so with the Shepherd. To him every face is different. Every face is a story. Every face is a child. Every child has a name.

The shepherd knows his sheep. He knows each one by name. The Shepherd knows you. He knows your name. And he will never forget it.

When God Whispers Your Name

Father, it is so good to know that we are not alone or lost in a crowd—your eyes are upon us in all that we do. You even know our thoughts! Thank you for the promise of your presence in our lives.

Inspirational Promises

The LORD searches all the earth for people who have given themselves completely to him. He wants to make them strong.

2 Chronicles 16:9

LORD, you are my shield, my wonderful God who gives me courage.

Psalm 3:3

The Lord is faithful and will give you strength and will protect you from the Evil One.

2 Thessalonians 3:3

I love the LORD, because he listens to my prayers for help. He paid attention to me, so I will call to him for help as long as I live.

Psalm 116:1

JESUS, OUR HOPE

Perhaps the heaviest burden we try to carry is the burden of mistakes and failures. What do you do with your failures?

Even if you've fallen, even if you've failed, even if everyone else has rejected you, Christ will not turn away from you. He came first and foremost to those who have no hope. He goes to those no one else would go to and says, "I'll give you eternity."

Only you can surrender your concerns to the Father. No one else can take those away and give them to God. Only you can cast all your anxieties on the one who cares for you. What better way to start the day than by laying your cares at his feet?

Walking with the Savior

Father, thank you that we aren't left to merely cope and grapple with yesterday's failures. Your mercies are new every morning. You give strength to the weary. You make us soar on wings like eagles. You are a mighty and wonderful God!

Praise be to the God and Father of our Lord Jesus Christ. In God's great mercy he has caused us to be born again into a living hope, because Jesus Christ rose from the dead.

1 Peter 1:3

Now I am right with God, not because I followed the law, but because I believed in Christ. God uses my faith to make me right with him. I want to know Christ and the power that raised him from the dead. . . . Then I have hope that I myself will be raised from the dead.

Philippians 3:9–11

These two things cannot change: God cannot lie when he makes a promise, and he cannot lie when he makes an oath. These things encourage us who came to God for safety. They give us strength to hold on to the hope we have been given. We have this hope as an anchor for the soul, sure and strong.

Hebrews 6:18–19

JESUS, OUR EXAMPLE

Is there any emotion that imprisons the soul more than the unwillingness to forgive? What do you do when people mistreat you or those you love? Does the fire of anger boil within you, with leaping flames consuming your emotions? Or do you reach somewhere, to some source of cool water and pull out a bucket of mercy—to free yourself?

Don't get on the roller coaster of resentment and anger. You be the one who says, "Yes, he mistreated me, but I am going to be like Christ. I'll be the one who says, 'Forgive them, Father; they don't know what they're doing.'"

Walking with the Savior

Father, forgiveness isn't a natural response toward someone who has hurt us. Help us to remember that we need forgiveness too, and that when we extend forgiveness toward others, we are the ones who are set free.

Inspirational Promises

If you suffer for doing good, and you are patient, then God is pleased. This is what you were called to do, because Christ suffered for you and gave you an example to follow. So you should do as he did.

1 Peter 2:20–21

When you do things, do not let selfishness or pride be your guide. Instead, be humble and give more honor to others than to yourselves. Do not be interested only in your own life, but be interested in the lives of others. In your lives you must think and act like Christ Jesus.

Philippians 2:3–5

"If I, your Lord and Teacher, have washed your feet, you also should wash each other's feet. I did this as an example so that you should do as I have done for you."

John 13:14–15

JESUS, THE GOOD SHEPHERD

Sheep aren't smart. They tend to wander into running creeks for water, then their wool grows heavy and they drown. They need a shepherd to lead them to "calm water" (Psalm 23:2). They have no natural defense—no claws, no horns, no fangs. They are helpless. Sheep need a shepherd with a "rod and . . . walking stick" (v. 4) to protect them. They have no sense of direction. They need someone to lead them "on paths that are right" (v. 3).

So do we. We, too, tend to be swept away by waters we should have avoided. We have no defense against the evil lion who prowls about, seeking who he might devour. We, too, get lost.

We need a shepherd. We need a shepherd to care for us and to guide us. And we have one. One who knows us by name.

A Gentle Thunder

Father, thank you for giving us a Shepherd to guide us, to feed us, to anoint us. A Shepherd who loves us and cares for us. Help us not to go astray but to follow him.

The LORD is my shepherd; I have everything I need. He lets me rest in green pastures. He leads me to calm water. He gives me new strength. He leads me on paths that are right for the good of his name.

Psalm 23:1–3

"I am the good shepherd. The good shepherd gives his life for the sheep. . . . I am the good shepherd. I know my sheep, and my sheep know me just as the Father knows me, and I know the Father. I give my life for the sheep."

John 10:11, 14–15

God raised from the dead our Lord Jesus, the Great Shepherd of the sheep, because of the blood of his death. His blood began the eternal agreement that God made with his people.

Hebrews 13:20–21

JESUS, OUR BURDEN-BEARER

When it comes to healing our spiritual condition, we don't have a chance. We might as well be told to pole-vault the moon. We don't have what it takes to be healed. Our only hope is that God will do for us what he did for the man at Bethesda—that he will step out of the temple and step into our ward of hurt and helplessness.

Which is exactly what he has done.

I wish we would take Jesus at his word.

When he says we're forgiven, let's unload the guilt.
When he says we're valuable, let's believe him.
When he says we're eternal, let's bury our fear.
When he says we're provided for, let's stop worrying.

God's efforts are strongest when our efforts are useless.

He Still Moves Stones

Lord, our needs are so great—we need your forgiveness, healing, redemption, and grace. We give you our state of weakness so that we can live in your power and strength.

Inspirational Promises

Give your worries to the Lord, and he will take care of you. He will never let good people down.

Psalm 55:22

But [the Lord] said to me, "My grace is enough for you. When you are weak, my power is made perfect in you." . . . For this reason I am happy when I have weaknesses, insults, hard times, sufferings, and all kinds of troubles for Christ. Because when I am weak, then I am truly strong.

2 Corinthians 12:9–10

I [Paul] pray also that the eyes of your heart may be enlightened in order that you may know the hope to which he has called you, the riches of his glorious inheritance in the saints, and his incomparably great power for us who believe.

Ephesians 1:18–19 NIV

JESUS, OUR SECURITY

You and I are on a great climb. The wall is high, and the stakes are higher. You took your first step the day you confessed Christ as the Son of God. He gave you his harness—the Holy Spirit. In your hands he placed a rope—his Word.

Your first steps were confident and strong, but with the journey came weariness, and with the height came fear. You lost your footing. You lost your focus. You lost your grip, and you fell. For a moment, which seemed like forever, you tumbled wildly. Out of control. Out of self-control. Disoriented. Dislodged. Falling.

But then the rope tightened, and the tumble ceased. You hung in the harness and found it to be strong. You grasped the rope and found it to be true. And though you can't see your guide, you know him. You know he is strong. You know he is able to keep you from falling.

A Gentle Thunder

Teach us to set our hopes on heaven, to hold firmly to the promises of your Word, so that we can withstand the struggles and storms of this world.

[God] is strong and can help you not to fall. He can bring you before his glory without any wrong in you and can give you great joy.

Jude v. 24

The Lord is faithful and will give you strength and will protect you from the Evil One.

2 Thessalonians 3:3

May our Lord Jesus Christ himself and God our Father encourage you and strengthen you in every good thing you do and say. God loved us, and through his grace he gave us a good hope and encouragement that continues forever.

2 Thessalonians 2:16–17

Now we hope for the blessings God has for his children. These blessings, which cannot be destroyed or be spoiled or lose their beauty, are kept in heaven for you. God's power protects you through your faith until salvation is shown to you at the end of time.

1 Peter 1:4–5

JESUS, OUR ETERNAL KING

The whole purpose of coming before the King is to praise him, to live in recognition of his splendor. Praise—lifting up our hearts and hands, exulting with our voices, singing his praises—is the occupation of those who dwell in the kingdom.

Praise is the highest occupation of any being. What happens when we praise the Father? We reestablish the proper chain of command; we recognize that the King is on the throne and that he has saved his people.

Walking with the Savior

Heavenly Father, you are our mighty God and we praise your holy name. It is because of you that we have life everlasting, and for this, we give you all glory and honor forever!

The LORD is our judge. The LORD makes our laws. The LORD is our king. He will save us.

Isaiah 33:22

I was given mercy so that in me, the worst of all sinners, Christ Jesus could show that he has patience without limit. His patience with me made me an example for those who would believe in him and have life forever. To the King that rules forever, who will never die, who cannot be seen, the only God, be honor and glory forever and ever.

1 Timothy 1:16–17

The One on the throne said to me, "It is finished. I am the Alpha and the Omega, the Beginning and the End. I will give free water from the spring of the water of life to anyone who is thirsty. Those who win the victory will receive this, and I will be their God, and they will be my children."

Revelation 21:6–7

Inspirational Promises When You Have Special Needs

BEING RIGHT BEFORE GOD

We are thirsty.

Not thirsty for fame, possessions, passion, or romance. We've drunk from those pools. They are salt water in the desert. They don't quench—they kill.

"Blessed are those who hunger and thirst for righteousness. . . ."

Righteousness. That's it. That's what we are thirsty for. We're thirsty for a clean conscience. We crave a clean slate. We yearn for a fresh start. We pray for a hand which will enter the dark cavern of our world and do for us the one thing we can't do for ourselves—make us right again.

The Applause of Heaven

Father, we are a ragged lot, bound together by broken dreams and collapsed promises. We come to you now, for only you can make us right again.

Love never hurts a neighbor, so loving is obeying all the law. Do this because we live in an important time. It is now time for you to wake up from your sleep, because our salvation is nearer now than when we first believed.

Romans 13:10–11

Now respect the LORD and serve him fully and sincerely. . . . Serve the LORD. But if you don't want to serve the LORD, you must choose for yourselves today whom you will serve.

Joshua 24:14–15

Jesus has the power of God, by which he has given us everything we need to live and to serve God. We have these things because we know him. Jesus called us by his glory and goodness. Through these he gave us the very great and precious promises. With these gifts you can share in God's nature, and the world will not ruin you with its evil desires.

2 Peter 1:3–4

FEARING DEATH

The problem with this world is that it doesn't fit. Oh, it will do for now, but it isn't tailor-made. We were made to live with God, but on earth we live by faith. We were made to live forever, but on this earth we live but for a moment.

We must trust God. We must trust not only that he does what is best but that he knows what is ahead. Ponder the words of Isaiah 57:1–2: "The good men perish; the godly die before their time and no one seems to care or wonder why. No one seems to realize that God is taking them away from the evil days ahead. For the godly who die shall rest in peace" (TLB).

My, what a thought. "God is taking them away from the evil days ahead." Could death be God's grace? Could the funeral wreath be God's safety ring? As horrible as the grave may be, could it be God's protection from the future?

Trust in God, Jesus urges, and trust in me.

A Gentle Thunder

Father, we know that someday you're going to take all your followers into eternal happiness. And it is to that day, Father, that we look. And it is upon our hope and confidence that you will return, that we stand.

When people are tempted and still continue strong, they should be happy. After they have proved their faith, God will reward them with life forever. God promised this to all those who love him.

James 1:12

This body that can be destroyed will clothe itself with that which can never be destroyed, and this body that dies will clothe itself with that which can never die. . . . Death's power to hurt is sin, and the power of sin is the law. But we thank God! He gives us the victory through our Lord Jesus Christ.

1 Corinthians 15:54, 56–57

We know that our body—the tent we live in here on earth—will be destroyed. But when that happens, God will have a house for us. It will not be a house made by human hands; instead, it will be a home in heaven that will last forever.

2 Corinthians 5:1

FEELING OVERWHELMED BY PROBLEMS

God's blessings are dispensed according to the riches of his grace, not according to the depth of our faith. "If we are not faithful, he will still be faithful, because he cannot be false to himself" (2 Timothy 2:13).

Why is that important to know? So you won't get cynical. Look around you. Aren't there more mouths than bread? Aren't there more wounds than physicians? Aren't there more who need the truth than those who tell it?

So what do we do? Throw up our hands and walk away? Tell the world we can't help them?

No, we don't give up. We look up. We trust. We believe. And our optimism is not hollow. Christ has proven worthy. He has shown that he never fails. That's what makes God, God.

A Gentle Thunder

Father, when we are weak, you are strong. When we have no faith, you are faithful. Thank you for being true to us even when we forget you.

Lord, *answer me because your love is so good. Because of your great kindness, turn to me. Do not hide from me, your servant. I am in trouble. Hurry to help me! Come near and save me; rescue me from my enemies.*

Psalm 69:16–18

I love the Lord, *because he listens to my prayers for help. He paid attention to me, so I will call to him for help as long as I live.*

Psalm 116:1–2

"I have good plans for you, not plans to hurt you. I will give you hope and a good future. Then you will call my name. You will come to me and pray to me, and I will listen to you. You will search for me. And when you search for me with all your heart, you will find me!"

Jeremiah 29:11–13

WHEN GOD SEEMS SILENT

Go back and report to John what you hear and see: "The blind receive sight, the lame walk . . . and the good news is preached to the poor."

This was Jesus' answer to John's agonized query from the dungeon of doubt: "Are you the one who was to come, or should we expect someone else?"

We don't know how John received Jesus' message, but we can imagine. I like to think of a slight smile coming over his lips as he heard what his Master said. For now he understood. It wasn't that Jesus was silent; it was that John had been listening for the wrong answer. John had been listening for an answer to his earthly problems, while Jesus was busy resolving his heavenly ones. That's worth remembering the next time you hear the silence of God.

The Applause of Heaven

Father, nothing is louder than the silence of our God. But, Father, forgive us for the times we've interpreted your silence as a lack of love. Give us patience, for we know you'll answer, Father, if only we'll wait.

Inspirational Promises

"Ask, and God will give to you. Search, and you will find. Knock, and the door will open for you. Yes, everyone who asks will receive. Everyone who searches will find. And everyone who knocks will have the door opened."

Matthew 7:7–8

Without faith no one can please God. Anyone who comes to God must believe that he is real and that he rewards those who truly want to find him.

Hebrews 11:6

This is the boldness we have in God's presence: that if we ask God for anything that agrees with what he wants, he hears us. If we know he hears us every time we ask him, we know we have what we ask from him.

1 John 5:14–15

LONGING FOR HEAVEN

The only ultimate disaster that can befall us, I have come to realize, is to feel ourselves to be home on earth. As long as we are aliens, we cannot forget our true homeland.

Unhappiness on earth cultivates a hunger for heaven. By gracing us with a deep dissatisfaction, God holds our attention. The only tragedy, then, is to be satisfied prematurely. To settle for earth. To be content in a strange land.

We are not happy here because we are not at home here. We are not happy here because we are not supposed to be happy here. We are "like foreigners and strangers in this world" (1 Peter 2:11).

And you will never be completely happy on earth simply because you were not made for earth. Oh, you will have moments of joy. You will catch glimpses of light. You will know moments or even days of peace. But they simply do not compare with the happiness that lies ahead.

When God Whispers Your Name

Father, our happiness lies ahead when we will be involved in the ongoing process of co-reigning with you.

I have no one in heaven but you; I want nothing on earth besides you. My body and my mind may become weak, but God is my strength. He is mine forever.

Psalm 73:25–26

"There are many rooms in my Father's house; I would not tell you this if it were not true. I am going there to prepare a place for you. After I go and prepare a place for you, I will come back and take you to be with me so that you may be where I am."

John 14:2–3

No one has ever seen this, and no one has ever heard about it. No one has ever imagined what God has prepared for those who love him.

1 Corinthians 2:9

STRUGGLING WITH WORLDLINESS

John the Baptist would never get hired today. No church would touch him. He was a public relations disaster. He "wore clothes made from camel's hair, had a leather belt around his waist, and ate locusts and wild honey" (Mark 1:6). Who would want to look at a guy like that every Sunday?

His message was as rough as his dress: a no-nonsense, bare-fisted challenge to repent because God was on his way.

John the Baptist set himself apart for one task, to be a voice of Christ. Everything about John centered on his purpose. His dress. His diet. His actions. His demands.

You don't have to be like the world to have an impact on the world. You don't have to be like the crowd to change the crowd. You don't have to lower yourself down to their level to lift them up to your level. Holiness doesn't seek to be odd. Holiness seeks to be like God.

A Gentle Thunder

Father, this world can be influential in all the wrong ways. Help us to stay focused on our purpose—to be witnesses of your love to a lost people.

Think only about the things in heaven, not the things on earth. Your old sinful self has died, and your new life is kept with Christ in God.

Colossians 3:2–3

You should know that loving the world is the same as hating God. Anyone who wants to be a friend of the world becomes God's enemy.

James 4:4

Do not love the world or the things in the world. If you love the world, the love of the Father is not in you. These are the ways of the world: wanting to please our sinful selves, wanting the sinful things we see, and being too proud of what we have. None of these come from the Father, but all of them come from the world. The world and everything that people want in it are passing away, but the person who does what God wants lives forever.

1 John 2:15–17

FEELING ANXIOUS
ABOUT GROWING OLD

Growing old can be dangerous. The trail is treacherous and the pitfalls are many. One is wise to be prepared. You know it's coming. It's not like God kept the process a secret. It's not like you are blazing a trail as you grow older. It's not as if no one has ever done it before. Look around you. You have ample opportunity to prepare and ample case studies to consider. If growing old catches you by surprise, don't blame God. He gave you plenty of warning. He also gave you plenty of advice.

Your last chapters can be your best. Your final song can be your greatest. It could be that all of your life has prepared you for a grand exit. God's oldest have always been among his choicest.

As we get older, our vision should improve. Not our vision of earth, but our vision of heaven.

He Still Moves Stones

Father, we remember the moment we first believed. The flame in our hearts was dancing so hot we knew even death couldn't put it out. Rekindle that flame in our hearts now as we near the point when we'll stand face-to-face with you, the only hope this earth knows.

"Even when you are old, I will be the same. Even when your hair has turned gray, I will take care of you. I made you and will take care of you. I will carry you and save you."

Isaiah 46:4

I was young, and now I am old, but I have never seen good people left helpless or their children begging for food.

Psalm 37:25

God, you have taught me since I was young. To this day I tell about the miracles you do. Even though I am old and gray, do not leave me, God. I will tell the children about your power; I will tell those who live after me about your might.

Psalm 71:17–18

STRIVING FOR POWER

The push for power has come to shove. And most of us are either pushing or being pushed.

I might point out the difference between a passion for excellence and a passion for power. The desire for excellence is a gift of God, much needed in society. It is characterized by respect for quality and a yearning to use God's gifts in a way that pleases him.

But there is a canyon of difference between doing your best to glorify God and doing whatever it takes to glorify yourself. The quest for excellence is a mark of maturity. The quest for power is childish.

A thousand years from now, will it matter what title the world gave you? No, but it will make a literal hell of a difference whose child you are.

The Applause of Heaven

Father, it's so easy to let pride creep into our actions and motives in our daily activities. Help us to have a passion for excellence so that you, and only you, will receive glory in all that we do.

Do not fool yourselves. If you think you are wise in this world, you should become a fool so that you can become truly wise, because the wisdom of this world is foolishness with God.

1 Corinthians 3:18–19

Where jealousy and selfishness are, there will be confusion and every kind of evil. But the wisdom that comes from God is first of all pure, then peaceful, gentle, and easy to please. This wisdom is always ready to help those who are troubled and to do good for others. It is always fair and honest.

James 3:16–17

All of you should be very humble with each other.

> *"God is against the proud,*
> *but he gives grace to the humble."* Proverbs 3:34

Be humble under God's powerful hand so he will lift you up when the right time comes.

1 Peter 5:5–6

FEELING INSECURE ABOUT YOURSELF

Antonio Stradivari was a seventeenth-century violin maker whose name in its Latin form, *Stradivarius*, has become synonymous with excellence. He once said that to make a violin less than his best would be to rob God, who could not make Antonio Stradivari's violins without Antonio.

He was right. God could not make Stradivarius violins without Antonio Stradivari. Certain gifts were given to that craftsman that no other violin maker possessed.

In the same vein, there are certain things you can do that no one else can. Perhaps it is parenting, or constructing houses, or encouraging the discouraged. There are things that *only* you can do, and you are alive to do them. In the great orchestra we call life, you have an instrument and a song, and you owe it to God to play them both sublimely.

The Applause of Heaven

Father, we belong to your eternal plan. May that thought motivate us. Renew our minds with the immovable fact that we are part of a commissioned people—we have a reason to be alive.

You made my whole being; you formed me in my mother's body. I praise you because you made me in an amazing and wonderful way. What you have done is wonderful. I know this very well.

Psalm 139:13–14

"Two sparrows cost only a penny, but not even one of them can die without your Father's knowing it. God even knows how many hairs are on your head. So don't be afraid. You are worth much more than many sparrows."

Matthew 10:29–31

You are God's children whom he loves, so try to be like him. Live a life of love just as Christ loved us and gave himself for us as a sweet-smelling offering and sacrifice to God.

Ephesians 5:1–2

Trying to Earn Salvation

The supreme force in salvation is God's grace. Not our works. Not our talents. Not our feelings. Not our strength.

Salvation is God's sudden, calming presence during the stormy seas of our lives. We hear his voice; we take the step.

We, like Paul, are aware of two things: We are great sinners and we need a great savior.

We, like Peter, are aware of two facts: We are going down and God is standing up. So we scramble out. We leave behind the *Titanic* of self-righteousness and stand on the solid path of God's grace.

And, surprisingly, we are able to walk on water. Death is disarmed. Failures are forgivable. Life has real purpose. And God is not only within sight; he is within reach.

In the Eye of the Storm

Father, your grace is amazing! There is no limit to it's healing power, no matter what we've done or what we're going through. Thank you for being a God of love that we can always turn to.

Since we have been made right with God by our faith, we have peace with God. This happened through our Lord Jesus Christ, who through our faith has brought us into that blessing of God's grace that we now enjoy. And we are happy because of the hope we have of sharing God's glory.

Romans 5:1–2

The wicked should stop doing wrong, and they should stop their evil thoughts. They should return to the LORD so he may have mercy on them. They should come to our God, because he will freely forgive them.

Isaiah 55:7

This is what God told us: God has given us eternal life, and this life is in his Son. Whoever has the Son has life, but whoever does not have the Son of God does not have life.

1 John 5:11–12

GOD'S PURPOSE FOR YOUR LIFE

It's easy to thank God when he does what we want. But God doesn't always do what we want. Ask Job.

His empire collapsed, his children were killed, and what was a healthy body became a rage of boils. From whence came this torrent? From whence will come any help?

Job goes straight to God and pleads his case. His head hurts. His body hurts. His heart hurts.

And God answers. Not with answers but with questions. An ocean of questions. . . .

After several dozen questions . . . Job is left on the beach—drenched and wide-eyed. . . . He has gotten the point. What is it?

The point is this: God owes no one anything. No reasons. No explanations. Nothing. If he gave them, we couldn't understand them.

God is God. He knows what he is doing. When you can't trace his hand, trust his heart.

The Inspirational Study Bible

Father, may our hearts fully trust that you are in control and that you will meet our every need.

INSPIRATIONAL PROMISES

The LORD says, "My thoughts are not like your thoughts. Your ways are not like my ways. Just as the heavens are higher than the earth, so are my ways higher than your ways and my thoughts higher than your thoughts."

Isaiah 55:8–9

"Don't worry and say, 'What will we eat?' or 'What will we drink?' or 'What will we wear?' The people who don't know God keep trying to get these things, and your Father in heaven knows you need them. Seek first God's kingdom and what God wants. Then all your other needs will be met as well."

Matthew 6:31–33

If we are not faithful, he will still be faithful, because he must be true to who he is. . . . God's strong foundation continues to stand. These words are written on the seal: "The Lord knows those who belong to him," and "Everyone who wants to belong to the Lord must stop doing wrong."

2 Timothy 2:13, 19

Inspirational Promises of Assurance

GOD WILL MEET
YOUR NEEDS

God's faithfulness has never depended on the faithfulness of his children. He is faithful even when we aren't. When we lack courage, he doesn't. He has made a history out of using people in spite of people.

Need an example? The feeding of the five thousand. It's the only miracle, aside from those of the final week, recorded in all four Gospels. Why did all four writers think it worth repeating? . . . Perhaps they wanted to show how God doesn't give up even when his people do.

When the disciples didn't pray, Jesus prayed. When the disciples didn't see God, Jesus sought God. When the disciples were weak, Jesus was strong. When the disciples had no faith, Jesus had faith.

I simply think God is greater than our weakness. In fact, I think it is our weakness that reveals how great God is.

God is faithful even when his children are not.

A Gentle Thunder

Father, may we remember that you can still the storms that rage within our hearts. You can calm the whirling winds of fear and hurt that threaten our faith. We just need to call on you!

INSPIRATIONAL PROMISES

The power of the wicked will be broken, but the LORD supports those who do right. The LORD watches over the lives of the innocent, and their reward will last forever. They will not be ashamed when trouble comes. They will be full in times of hunger.

Psalm 37:17–19

"All that the Father has is mine. . . . I tell you the truth, my Father will give you anything you ask for in my name. Until now you have not asked for anything in my name. Ask and you will receive, so that your joy will be the fullest possible joy."

John 16:15, 23–24

My God will use his wonderful riches in Christ Jesus to give you everything you need.

Philippians 4:19

GOD WANTS YOU TO
BELONG TO HIM

For all its peculiarities and unevenness, the Bible has a simple story. God made man. Man rejected God. God won't give up until he wins man back.

God will whisper. He will shout. He will touch and tug. He will take away our burdens; he'll even take away our blessings. If there are a thousand steps between us and him, he will take all but one. But he will leave the final one for us. The choice is ours.

Please understand. His goal is not to make you happy. His goal is to make you his. His goal is not to get you what you want; it is to get you what you need.

A Gentle Thunder

Father, may we step into your arms each and every day and choose to serve you, no matter your will for our lives.

My whole being, praise the LORD and do not forget all his kindnesses. He forgives all my sins and heals all my diseases. He saves my life from the grave and loads me with love and mercy.

Psalm 103:2–4

The LORD your God is with you; the mighty One will save you. He will rejoice over you. You will rest in his love; he will sing and be joyful about you.

Zephaniah 3:17

The important thing is obeying God's commands. . . . You all were bought at a great price, so do not become slaves of people.

1 Corinthians 7:19, 23

God's Love Is Constant

A lot of us live with a hidden fear that God is angry at us. Somewhere, sometime, some Sunday school class or some television show convinced us that God has a whip behind his back, a paddle in his back pocket, and he's going to nail us when we've gone too far.

No concept could be more wrong! Our Savior's Father is very fond of us and only wants to share his love with us.

We have a Father who is filled with compassion, a feeling Father who hurts when his children hurt. We serve a God who says that even when we're under pressure and feel like nothing is going to go right, he is waiting for us, to embrace us whether we succeed or fail.

He doesn't come quarreling and wrangling and forcing his way into anyone's heart. He comes into our hearts like a gentle lamb, not a roaring lion.

Walking with the Savior

We thank you for your constant love, Father. Your love is not based on feelings or perfection but on your covenant with your people. Nothing can separate us from your love.

Inspirational Promises

God, you are my God. I search for you. I thirst for you like someone in a dry, empty land where there is no water. . . . Because your love is better than life, I will praise you.

Psalm 63:1, 3

Lord, you are kind and forgiving and have great love for those who call to you.

Psalm 86:5

Where God's love is, there is no fear, because God's perfect love drives out fear. It is punishment that makes a person fear, so love is not made perfect in the person who fears. We love because God first loved us.

1 John 4:18–19

GOD ENABLES YOU TO LIVE VICTORIOUSLY

You get impatient with your own life, trying to master a habit or control a sin—and in your frustration begin to wonder where the power of God is. Be patient. God is using today's difficulties to strengthen you for tomorrow. He is *equipping* you. The God who makes things grow will help you bear fruit.

Dwell on the fact that God lives within you. Think about the power that gives you life. The realization that God is dwelling within you may change the places you want to go and the things you want to do today.

Do what is right this week. Whatever it is, whatever comes down the path, whatever problems and dilemmas you face—just do what's right. Maybe no one else is doing what's right, but you do what's right. You be honest. You take a stand. You be true. After all, regardless of what you do, God does what is right: he saves you with his grace.

Walking with the Savior

Father, we long to be victorious disciples. Help us as we seek to have a clear head and a pure heart. May your Word and your power bring victory to our lives.

Know that the LORD is God. He made us, and we belong to him; we are his people, the sheep he tends.

Psalm 100:3

The LORD gives strength to his people; the LORD blesses his people with peace.

Psalm 29:11

Live in the right way, serve God, have faith, love, patience, and gentleness. Fight the good fight of faith, grabbing hold of the life that continues forever. You were called to have that life when you confessed the good confession before many witnesses.

1 Timothy 6:11–12

This is the victory that conquers the world—our faith. So the one who conquers the world is the person who believes that Jesus is the Son of God.

1 John 5:4–5

God Is in Control

We need to hear that God is still in control. We need to hear that it's not over until he says so. We need to hear that life's mishaps and tragedies are not a reason to bail out. They are simply a reason to sit tight.

Corrie ten Boom used to say, "When the train goes through a tunnel and the world gets dark, do you jump out? Of course not. You sit still and trust the engineer to get you through." . . .

Next time you're disappointed, don't panic. Don't jump out. Don't give up. Just be patient and let God remind you he's still in control. It ain't over till it's over.

He Still Moves Stones

Father, life can get so hard and circumstances so overwhelming. Help us not to panic and to remember that you reign. You are in control of the smallest details and will never leave us or forsake us.

INSPIRATIONAL PROMISES

The LORD is my light and the one who saves me. So why should I fear anyone? The LORD protects my life. So why should I be afraid?

Psalm 27:1

"I am the LORD, the God of every person on the earth. Nothing is impossible for me."

Jeremiah 32:27

"The mountains may disappear, and the hills may come to an end, but my love will never disappear; my promise of peace will not come to an end."

Isaiah 54:10

GOD EXALTS HUMILITY

I am frightened by our ability in America to convince ourselves that we don't need Jesus. We can amass fortunes, we can get degrees, we can own our house all on our own. And yet there's a certain affluence that we can attain when we become poverty-stricken—a certain humility that comes with trials, that brings us face-to-face with the Savior.

Revealing our feelings is the beginning of healing. Articulating what's on our heart, confessing our mistakes, is the first step in seeing that God can forgive those mistakes and all others.

God exalts humility. When God works in our lives, helping us to become humble, he gives us a permanent joy: humility gives us a joy that cannot be taken away.

Walking with the Savior

Holy Father, we need you! There isn't anything in this life on this earth that we can do without your love and your grace at work within us. May we never forget our dependence on you.

"Whoever makes himself great will be made humble. Whoever makes himself humble will be made great."

Matthew 23:12

Always be humble, gentle, and patient, accepting each other in love. You are joined together with peace through the Spirit, so make every effort to continue together in this way.

Ephesians 4:2

God is against the proud, but he gives grace to the humble.

James 4:6

Then [Jesus] said, "I tell you the truth, you must change and become like little children. Otherwise, you will never enter the kingdom of heaven. The greatest person in the kingdom of heaven is the one who makes himself humble like this child."

Matthew 18:3–4

GOD BLESSES
PURSUIT OF HIM

The most powerful life is the most simple life. The most powerful life is the life that knows where it's going, that knows where the source of strength is, and the life that stays free of clutter and happenstance and hurriedness.

Being busy is not a sin. Jesus was busy. Paul was busy. Peter was busy. Nothing of significance is achieved without effort and hard work and weariness. Being busy, in and of itself, is not a sin. But being busy in an endless pursuit of *things* that leave us empty and hollow and broken inside—that cannot be pleasing to God.

One source of man's weariness is the pursuit of things that can never satisfy; but which one of us has not been caught up in that pursuit at some time in our life? Our passions, possessions, and pride—these are all *dead* things. When we try to get life out of dead things, the result is only weariness and dissatisfaction.

Walking with the Savior

Father, remind us that in the midst of our busyness, the cross is still there. In the midst of our emptiness, the cross is still there. With your promises, Father, we can claim peace in the midst of our hectic lives.

Wait and trust the LORD. Don't be upset when others get rich or when someone else's plans succeed. Don't get angry. Don't be upset; it only leads to trouble.

Psalm 37:7–8

"Don't store treasures for yourselves here on earth where moths and rust will destroy them and thieves can break in and steal them. But store your treasures in heaven where they cannot be destroyed by moths or rust and where thieves cannot break in and steal them. Your heart will be where your treasure is."

Matthew 6:19–21

Command those who are rich with things of this world not to be proud. Tell them to hope in God, not in their uncertain riches. God richly gives us everything to enjoy. Tell the rich people to do good, to be rich in doing good deeds, to be generous and ready to share.

1 Timothy 6:17–18

God Honors Integrity

Only the holy will see God. Holiness is a prerequisite to heaven. Perfection is a requirement for eternity. We wish it weren't so. We act like it isn't so. We act like those who are decent will see God. We suggest that those who try hard will see God. We act as if we're good if we never do anything too bad. And that goodness is enough to qualify us for heaven.

Sounds right to us, but it doesn't sound right to God. And he sets the standard. And the standard is high. "You must be perfect, just as your Father in heaven is perfect" (Matthew 5:48).

You see, in God's plan, God is the standard for perfection. We don't compare ourselves to others; they are just as fouled up as we are. The goal is to be like him; anything less is inadequate.

He Still Moves Stones

Father, create in us a constant desire for righteousness and wisdom. And may our complete joy come from pleasing you in all that we do.

A wise person will understand what to do, but a foolish person is dishonest. Fools don't care if they sin, but honest people work at being right.

Proverbs 14:8–9

If people please God, God will give them wisdom, knowledge, and joy. But sinners will get only the work of gathering and storing wealth that they will have to give to the ones who please God. So all their work is useless, like chasing the wind.

Ecclesiastes 2:26

Dear friends, you are like foreigners and strangers in this world. I beg you to avoid the evil things your bodies want to do that fight against your soul.

1 Peter 2:11

Inspirational
Promises About
the Christian Life

SIN

It wasn't the Romans who nailed Jesus to the cross. It wasn't spikes that held Jesus to the cross. What held him to that cross was his conviction that it was necessary that he become sin—that he who is pure become sin and that the wrath of God be poured down, not upon the creation, but upon the Creator.

When the one who knew no sin became sin for us, when the sinless one was covered with all the sins of all the world, God didn't call his army of angels to save him. He didn't, because he knew he would rather give up his Son than give up on us.

Regardless of what you've done, it's not too late. Regardless of how far you've fallen, it's not too late. It doesn't matter how low the mistake is; it's not too late to dig down, pull out that mistake and then let it go—and be free.

What makes a Christian a Christian is not perfection but forgiveness.

Walking with the Savior

Father, thank you for taking on the sins of this world so that we would be free—free of guilt and separation from you. Because of Jesus' death on the cross we now have the promise of spending eternity with you.

Sin came into the world because of what one man did, and with sin came death. This is why everyone must die—because everyone sinned. . . . One man disobeyed God, and many became sinners. In the same way, one man obeyed God, and many will be made right.

Romans 5:12, 19

Christ had no sin, but God made him become sin so that in Christ we could become right with God.

2 Corinthians 5:21

Christ himself suffered for sins once. He was not guilty, but he suffered for those who are guilty to bring you to God. His body was killed, but he was made alive in the spirit.

1 Peter 3:18

SALVATION

Tolerance. A prized virtue today. The ability to be understanding of those with whom you differ is a sign of sophistication. Jesus, too, was a champion of tolerance:

> Tolerant of the disciples when they doubted
> Tolerant of the crowds when they misunderstood
> Tolerant of us when we fall

But there is one area where Jesus was intolerant. There was one area where he was unindulgent and dogmatic.

As far as he was concerned, when it comes to salvation, there aren't several roads . . . there is only one road. . . . There aren't several paths . . . there is only one path. And that path is Jesus himself.

That is why it is so hard for people to believe in Jesus. It's much easier to consider him one of several options rather than the option. But such a philosophy is no option.

A Gentle Thunder

Lord, you are the way and the truth to life everlasting. May we be a living testimony to the lost so that they will find salvation through you.

Everyone has sinned and fallen short of God's glorious standard, and all need to be made right with God by his grace, which is a free gift. They need to be made free from sin through Jesus Christ.

Romans 3:23–24

If anyone does sin, we have a helper in the presence of the Father—Jesus Christ, the One who does what is right. He died in our place to take away our sins, and not only our sins but the sins of all people.

1 John 2:1–2

"God did not send his Son into the world to judge the world guilty, but to save the world through him. People who believe in God's Son are not judged guilty. . . . Those who believe in the Son have eternal life, but those who do not obey the Son will never have life. God's anger stays on them."

John 3:17–18, 36

REPENTANCE

If we confess our sins . . ." The biggest word in Scriptures just might be that two letter one, *if*. For confessing sins—admitting failure—is exactly what prisoners of pride refuse to do.

"Me a sinner? Oh sure, I get rowdy every so often, but I'm a pretty good ol' boy."

"Listen, I'm just as good as the next guy. I pay my taxes. . . ."

Justification. Rationalization. Comparison. . . . They sound good. They sound familiar. They even sound American. But in the kingdom, they sound hollow.

When you get to the point of sorrow for your sins, when you admit that you have no other option . . . then cast all your cares on him, for he is waiting.

The Applause of Heaven

Father, it's easy to avoid confessing our sins. It's difficult looking at any wrong we've done. Yet, as soon as we repent, we are forgiven—you keep no record of wrongs. Help us to remember that repentance brings freedom!

186

Inspirational Truths

Then I confessed my sins to you and didn't hide my guilt. I said, "I will confess my sins to the Lord," and you forgave my guilt.

Psalm 32:5

Change your hearts and lives and be baptized, each one of you, in the name of Jesus Christ for the forgiveness of your sins. And you will receive the gift of the Holy Spirit.

Acts 2:38

"I tell you there is more joy in heaven over one sinner who changes his heart and life, than over ninety-nine good people who don't need to change."

Luke 15:7

ETERNAL LIFE

"A time is coming when all who are dead and in their graves will hear his voice. Then they will come out of their graves. Those who did good will rise and have life forever, but those who did evil will rise to be judged guilty" (John 5:28–29).

Interesting. A day is coming when everyone will hear his voice. A day is coming when all the other voices will be silenced; his voice—and his voice only—will be heard.

Some will hear his voice for the very first time. It's not that he never spoke, it's just that they never listened. For these, God's voice will be the voice of a stranger. They will hear it once—and never hear it again. They will spend eternity fending off the voices they followed on earth.

But others will be called from their graves by a familiar voice. For they are sheep who know their Shepherd. They are servants who opened the door when Jesus knocked.

In the Eye of the Storm

Remind us, Father, that the most important thing we can do on this earth is reach out and help those who have not yet found the key to that life that is to come—eternal life with you.

Inspirational Truths

"I tell you the truth, whoever hears what I say and believes in the One who sent me has eternal life. That person will not be judged guilty but has already left death and entered life."

John 5:24

"I tell you the truth, whoever believes has eternal life."

John 6:47

"My sheep listen to my voice; I know them, and they follow me. I give them eternal life, and they will never die, and no one can steal them out of my hand. My Father gave my sheep to me. He is greater than all, and no person can steal my sheep out of my Father's hand."

John 10:27–29

SANCTIFICATION

I wonder if Jesus doesn't muster up a slight smile as he sees his lost sheep come straggling into the fold—the beaten, broken, dirty sheep who stands at the door, looking up at the Shepherd, asking, "Can I come in? I don't deserve it, but is there room in your kingdom for one more?" The Shepherd looks down at the sheep and says, "Come in. This is your home."

Salvation is the process that's done, that's secure, that no one can take away from you. Sanctification is the life-long process of being changed from one degree of glory to the next, growing in Christ, putting away the old, taking on the new.

The psalmist David would tell us that those who have been redeemed will say so! If we're not saying so, perhaps it's because we've forgotten what it is like to be redeemed. Let the redeemed of the earth say so!

Walking with the Savior

Father, thank you for not waiting until we have our moral life in order before you start loving us. Help us live worthy of your love, putting on more and more of the new life in Christ.

If people's thinking is controlled by the sinful self, there is death. But if their thinking is controlled by the Spirit, there is life and peace. When people's thinking is controlled by the sinful self, they are against God, because they refuse to obey God's law and really are not even able to obey God's law. Those people who are ruled by their sinful selves cannot please God.

Romans 8:6–8

We all show the Lord's glory, and we are being changed to be like him. This change in us brings ever greater glory, which comes from the Lord, who is the Spirit.

2 Corinthians 3:18

Surely you know that the people who do wrong will not inherit God's kingdom. . . . In the past, some of you were like that, but you were washed clean. You were made holy, and you were made right with God in the name of the Lord Jesus Christ and in the Spirit of our God.

1 Corinthians 6:9, 11

Prayer

You wonder if it is a blessing or a curse to have a mind that never rests. But you would rather be a cynic than a hypocrite, so you continue to pray with one eye open and wonder:

> about starving children
> about the power of prayer
> about Christians in cancer wards . . .

Tough questions. Throw-in-the-towel questions. Questions the disciples must have asked in the storm.

All they could see were black skies as they bounced in the battered boat.

A figure came to them walking on the water. It wasn't what they expected. . . . They almost missed seeing the answer to their prayers.

And unless we look and listen closely, we risk making the same mistake. God's lights in our dark nights are as numerous as the stars, if only we'll look for them.

In the Eye of the Storm

We come to you in prayer, Father. We don't know the answers to the whys. We depend on you. We don't know all the answers, but we know who knows the answers.

INSPIRATIONAL TRUTHS

"When you pray, you should go into your room and close the door and pray to your Father who cannot be seen. Your Father can see what is done in secret, and he will reward you."

Matthew 6:6

"If you ask for anything in my name, I will do it for you so that the Father's glory will be shown through the Son. If you ask me for anything in my name, I will do it."

John 14:13–14

In Christ we can come before God with freedom and without fear. We can do this through faith in Christ.

Ephesians 3:12

I tell you to pray for all people, asking God for what they need and being thankful to him. . . . I want the men everywhere to pray, lifting up their hands in a holy manner. . . .

1 Timothy 2:1, 8

LIVING LIKE CHRIST

Sacred delight is good news coming through the back door of your heart. It's what you'd always dreamed but never expected.

It is sacred because only God can grant it. It is a delight because it thrills.

It is this sacred delight that Jesus promises in the Sermon on the Mount.

And he promises it to an unlikely crowd: "The poor in spirit . . . Those who mourn . . . The meek . . . Those who hunger and thirst . . . The merciful . . . The pure in heart . . . The peacemakers . . . The persecuted . . ."

It is to this band of pilgrims that God promises a special blessing. A heavenly joy. A sacred delight.

The Applause of Heaven

Father, we want to experience your sacred delight! We want to be more like Christ! May we be steadfast in using the spiritual gifts you've given us, and remember the blessings that await when we do.

Inspirational Truths

"You are the light that gives light to the world. A city that is built on a hill cannot be hidden. And people don't hide a light under a bowl. They put it on a lampstand so the light shines for all the people in the house. In the same way, you should be a light for other people. Live so that they will see the good things you do and will praise your Father in heaven."

Matthew 5:14–16

This work must continue until we are all joined together in the same faith and in the same knowledge of the Son of God. We must become like a mature person, growing until we become like Christ and have his perfection.

Ephesians 4:13

Anyone who speaks should speak words from God. Anyone who serves should serve with the strength God gives so that in everything God will be praised through Jesus Christ. Power and glory belong to him forever and ever.

1 Peter 4:11

THE BODY OF CHRIST

In the third century, St. Cyprian wrote to a friend named Donatus:

> This seems a cheerful world, Donatus, when I view it from this fair garden. . . . But if I climbed some great mountain and looked out . . . you know very well what I would see; brigands on the high road, pirates on the seas, in the amphitheaters men murdered to please the applauding crowds. . . .
>
> Yet in the midst of it, I have found a quiet and holy people. . . . They are despised and persecuted, but they care not. They have overcome the world. These people, Donatus, are Christians. . . .

What a compliment! A *quiet and holy people.*

Quiet. . . . Not obnoxious. Not boastful. Not demanding. Just quiet.

Holy. . . . Set apart. Pure. Decent. Honest. Wholesome.

The Inspirational Study Bible

Father, help us to remember that oftentimes a quiet answer will draw more attention to your holiness than endless chatter. May our actions and words toward others be of peace, humility, and gentleness.

Inspirational Truths

A person's body is one thing, but it has many parts. Though there are many parts to a body, all those parts make only one body. Christ is like that also. . . . We were all baptized into one body through one Spirit. And we were all made to share in the one Spirit.

1 Corinthians 12:12–13

Let the teaching of Christ live in you richly. Use all wisdom to teach and instruct each other by singing psalms, hymns, and spiritual songs with thankfulness in your hearts to God. Everything you do or say should be done to obey Jesus your Lord. And in all you do, give thanks to God the Father through Jesus.

Colossians 3:16–17

You are a chosen people, royal priests, a holy nation, a people for God's own possession. You were chosen to tell about the wonderful acts of God, who called you out of darkness into his wonderful light.

1 Peter 2:9

DISCIPLESHIP

Watch a small boy follow his dad through the snow. He stretches to step where his dad stepped. Not an easy task. His small legs extend as far as they can so his feet can fall in his father's prints.

The father, seeing what the son is doing, smiles and begins taking shorter steps, so the son can follow.

It's a picture of discipleship.

In our faith we follow in someone's steps. A parent, a teacher, a hero—none of us are the first to walk the trail. All of us have someone we follow.

In our faith we leave footprints to guide others. A child, a friend, a recent convert. None should be left to walk the trail alone.

It's the principle of discipleship.

The Inspirational Study Bible

Father, may we be ever mindful of the impressions we are leaving for someone else to follow. And may they lead directly toward you.

"All people will know that you are my followers if you love each other."

John 13:35

"If you continue to obey my teaching, you are truly my followers. Then you will know the truth, and the truth will make you free."

John 8:31–32

"You should produce much fruit and show that you are my followers, which brings glory to my Father."

John 15:8

Heaven

What is more beautiful than a bride? . . . Maybe it is the aura of whiteness that clings to her as dew clings to a rose. Or perhaps it is the diamonds that glisten in her eyes. Or maybe it's the blush of love that pinks her cheeks or the bouquet of promises she carries.

A bride. A commitment robed in elegance. "I'll be with you forever." Tomorrow bringing hope today. Promised purity faithfully delivered.

When you read that our heavenly home is similar to a bride, tell me, doesn't it make you want to go home?

The Applause of Heaven

Father, we are glad to follow Christ. We have died to self. The life that we possess now is the life to come, not the life on this earth. With joy we look forward to spending all of eternity with you!

Inspirational Truths

The Lord has set his throne in heaven, and his kingdom rules over everything.

Psalm 103:19

You have this faith and love because of your hope, and what you hope for is kept safe for you in heaven. You learned about this hope when you heard the message about the truth, the Good News that was told to you.

Colossians 1:5–6

"People will insult you and hurt you. They will lie and say all kinds of evil things about you because you follow me. But when they do, you will be blessed. Rejoice and be glad, because you have a great reward waiting for you in heaven."

Matthew 5:11–12

Acknowledgments

Grateful acknowledgment is made to the following publishers for permission to reprint this copyrighted material. All copyrights are held by the author, Max Lucado.

The Applause of Heaven (Nashville: Word, 1990).
In the Eye of the Storm (Nashville: Word, 1991).
He Still Moves Stones (Nashville: Word, 1993).
Walking with the Savior (Wheaton: Tyndale House, 1993).
When God Whispers Your Name (Nashville: Word, 1994).
A Gentle Thunder (Nashville: Word, 1995).
The Inspirational Study Bible (Nashville: W Publishing Group, 1995).